William Bonin:

Most The True Story of The Freeway Killer

by Jack Rosewood

Historical Serial Killers and Murderers

True Crime by Evil Killers

Volume 10

Copyright © 2015 by Wiq Media

ALL RIGHTS RESERVED

No part of this book may be reproduced, stored in a retrieval system, or transmitted in any form or by any means, electronic, mechanical, photocopying, recording, scanning, or otherwise, without the prior written permission of the publisher.

ISBN-13: 978-1519631190

Table of Contents

Introduction 1

CHAPTER 1: Setting murderous future in stone 4

    Sexual assaults erase a childhood 5

    California dreamin' 7

    Something triggers string of assaults 9

    A wrong-way ride 11

    Back to prison 12

    First murder reveals degree of depravity 14

    A careless slip puts 20 boys in danger 16

    Vacation becomes date with death 17

    Brutality doesn't quell hunger 18

CHAPTER 2: William Bonin was hungry 20

    A sick Christmas gift 22

    A grisly New Year's celebration 23

    The unluckiest boy on earth 25

    Close call leads to new 'friend' 26

    Pugh becomes Bonin's latest accomplice 27

    Kills become big, big thrills 28

    Bodies of boys pile up 30

CHAPTER 3: Orange County Register unearths Bonin's secrets 31

    A profile of murder.. 32

    The story breaks 34

CHAPTER 4: Bonin's trail of death, torture continues 37

    Torture methods escalate 38

CHAPTER 5: A consummate serial killer 40

    Bonin knows no boundaries 42

    A solo killing leaves victim's family in turmoil 43

    Homeless man becomes Bonin's new roommate – and accomplice 44

    Story doesn't bypass Bonin's attention 44

    The last victim 48

    'I'll kill you if you run' 51

    An unfortunate miss.. 52

    Capture and confession.. 53

    Tricked into talking 54

    An encounter with the devil 55

    Butts lands behind bars 59

    Second accomplice arrested... 60

    Another accomplice lands in jail... 61

Fourth accomplice catches a break 63

Bonin enters innocent plea..64

A remorseless killer 65

Butts chooses suicide over facing the music 66

CHAPTER 6: The trials of William Bonin.............................. 69

Los Angeles trial..69

Reporter goes against tradition 71

Defending a madman 74

Closing arguments 75

Bonin's first death sentence 77

Orange County trial 78

Bonin uses up all his appeals 83

Accomplices also pay..86

Public defender tries to get death penalty off table 90

Do they play cards in hell?..91

CHAPTER 7: The execution of William Bonin 93

Lethal injection replaces gas chamber................................93

Bonin's death day comes..95

Last-minute fight for a stay...96

His last meal 97

Editorial protests empathy for Bonin 99

Witnesses anticipate justice 101

Rape victim relishes his chance at retribution 102

Execution 103

Not enough satisfaction 105

The aftermath 108

CHAPTER 8: Bonin's terror lives on 113

Secrets went to the grave 113

DA searches for DNA to complete Bonin's sordid portfolio 114

Mother reaps financial bounty during Bonin incarceration 115

The other Freeway Killers 116

A movie merges truth, fiction 117

Conclusion 118

A Note From The Author 120

Introduction

"Most people are overconfident of their value on this planet. Most people can be done without," said William George Bonin.

Overconfident of their value? William Bonin sure was.

He must have felt absolutely certain that police would never connect him to the string of dead bodies turning up along California's most picturesque highways, the blood-soaked and battered discoveries horribly juxtaposed against bright blue skies and roads with rock-lined ocean views.

But good eventually catches up with evil, if given enough time. And Bonin's obsession with brutal sex and murder was consuming him much too fast for him not to make a few mistakes.

Bonin was eventually caught and executed in 1996 for the callous, brutal killing at least 21 boys and young men during a fast-paced murder spree that ran from 1979 to 1980.

Human life didn't matter to Bonin. People could be thrown away like so much trash, completely forgotten in the hunt for a new victim.

And while most parents worry about their daughters, and warn them to take precautions, they usually forget that one third of all murder victims are male.

In the 1970s, it was boys who were dying with increased regularity along the highways and byways of southern California.

That's where Bonin trolled for his victims along the freeways, earning the nickname the Freeway Killer. It is one he shares with two other serial killers, Patrick Kearney and Randy Steven Kraft, who also took advantage of the busy and often anonymous California freeway system to procure their human playthings.

Bonin drove a camo green Ford Econoline camper van, and often used accomplices to either help entice his victims into the van and drive while he raped, tortured and killed them in the back or to assist him in the actual killing.

Bonin - despite being divorced - liked boys, and he liked them young. He targeted hitchhikers — most often thin and lanky types, although some of his younger victims were quite small - and sometimes lured kids to their deaths with the promise of sex and drugs. Sometimes he just overpowered them, forcing them into the back of the van where they would find door handles removed so they could not escape.

Once he had them, though, they were little more than toys to him, and he brutally raped and tortured them before killing them and discarding them with all the emotion of disposing of garbage.

He drove he "death van" around the streets of Los Angeles and Orange counties looking for victims, a prosecutor later said, adding that once a hitchhiker had entered Bonin's van "he was dead."

According to one accomplice, Bonin liked to hear them scream – and later, after everything came to light in horrible detail, neighbors would report having heard "blood-curdling screams" coming from the 1950s tract house in Downey where Bonin had spent his high school years and now shared with his mother.

At the time, they thought it was kids playing, so no 911 calls were made, even though neighbors had seen young boys with Bonin, which made them suspicious, and had heard rumors that Bonin was buying beer and showing porn to neighborhood teens.

But for a few mistakes, including choosing his accomplices based on lust, Bonin was on his way to becoming the most prolific serial killer of all time.

And to the families of those he sadistically murdered after torturing and raping them, Bonin was the one the world could have done without.

He was a monster from childhood.

CHAPTER 1:
Setting murderous future in stone

Born January 8, 1947 – the same day as futuristic musician David Bowie – William George Bonin's birthday came with a touch of irony. Victor Hugo's "Les Miserables" starring Frederic March and Charles Laughton was playing that day, and Bonin would later hunt down young boys with the same fervor that pushed the detective Javert to chase Jean Valjean in that classic story.

The second of three brothers, Bonin's Connecticut childhood was not full of Cape Cod charm. In truth, his parents were both drunks and his father had a pretty serious gambling problem that often consumed the family's grocery money, and eventually led to the foreclosure of their house. Neighbors who noticed the boys' hunger often came to the rescue.

The children gobbled, those Good Samaritan neighbors said, and were seemingly so hungry that they couldn't get the food into their mouths fast enough.

When things became particularly desperate for the parents, they left the boys with their maternal grandfather, a convicted child molester who had abused his daughter and most certainly abused his grandsons as well.

Sexual assaults erase a childhood

By the age of six, Bonin was in an orphanage, and although he later said he had no memories of the place, others who spent time there said that cruel punishments doled out by the facility's workers included having their heads shoved into toilet bowls and being forced to climb stairs until their legs wobbled and shook.

Bonin was just 10 when he was placed in a Connecticut juvenile detention center for stealing license plates. He was sexually assaulted that same year, apparently more than once and by more than one person, which likely led at least in part to his later obsession with sex and violence.

After he was sexually assaulted while housed in the detention center, he in turn molested his brothers and neighborhood boys, although his gruesome, bloody trek through southern California was still more than a decade in the future.

He was following a common pattern, experts say.

An estimated 35 percent of those who molest or sexually assault others were victims of some form of abuse themselves.

The cycle of shifting roles from victim to abuser – sometimes known as vampire syndrome - is especially common in pedophiles whose preferred targets are boys.

Once, when an older boy asked Bonin for sex, he was agreeable, as long as he were restrained with his wrists behind his back, a submissive position that he said made him feel more secure.

When psychologists heard the story, they said it suggested that Bonin had most certainly been a victim of sexual abuse by adults who had restrained the boy long before his stint in the detention center. His mother pointed her finger at grandpa, but given that Bonin had been essentially passed around among many of the older boys in the detention center, it would be hard to pinpoint what particularly incident triggered his own perverse desires.

According to a study appearing in the British Journal of Psychology, there are several factors that point to why people become perpetrators of sexual abuse.

Not only are boys who are victims of childhood sexual abuse more likely to become perpetrators themselves, but so are children who suffer abandonment from their parents during critical periods of development.

"Having been a victim was a strong predictor of becoming a perpetrator, as was an index of parental loss in childhood," researchers said.

William Bonin had both things working against him, and at least 21 young men and boys would be the ones who would pay for it, in the worst possible way.

California dreamin'

When Bonin was in 8th grade - their house foreclosed on and the future in Connecticut looking quite bleak - the family moved to California, hoping that the Golden State and all its promise would be the catalyst to transform their lives.

And while it may have been a good move for Bonin's parents and two brothers, the change in scenery did nothing to erase Bonin's increasingly dark thoughts.

Bonin had a lack of self-control, and his urges always got the best of him.

"Sometimes... I'd get tense and think I was gonna go crazy if I couldn't get some release, like my head would explode. So I'd go out hunting. Killing helped me... It was like ... needing to go gambling or getting drunk. I had to do it," Bonin said in Dr. Vonda Pelto's book "Without Remorse." (Pelto was a young clinical psychologist when she was given the job of preventing inmates from committing suicide before trial. One of her charges was Bonin.)

His victims dumped like garbage in the ditches alongside the freeways of southern California, Bonin was like so many other serial killers – habitual and unable to control his actions. The desire to kill was all-encompassing, and like a heroin addict in need of a fix, it was all he really thought about.

But we're getting a little ahead of ourselves.

There was a time when the paunchy, morose, dark-haired Bonin had a shot at living a normal life. If only those pesky little obsessions hadn't taken hold.

1965 was actually a good year for Bonin. He graduated from high school, got engaged to a girl and joined the U.S. Air Force.

He ended up in Vietnam, serving his time as an aerial gunner and logging more than 700 hours of combat and patrol time. He earned a Good Conduct Medal, and put his own life at risk to save a fellow airman.

On the surface, everything looked great, but despite his alleged "Good Conduct," he made the Vietnam War even more of a hell for two fellow soldiers when he sexually assaulted them at gunpoint. As if the humid, dense jungle, tricky Vietnamese booby traps and watching fellow squadron members being blown to pieces in plain sight weren't hell enough.

Later, at his Los Angeles County trial, the prosecutor would say, "the closest the defendant got to combat in Vietnam was when he held a gun to two soldiers' heads and sodomized them."

He was honorably discharged in 1968 – it wasn't until much later that he admitted the assaults, and his victims were unlikely to report such a thing during that era – and returned to California to live with his mother in Downey, located in Los Angeles County, about 13 miles southeast of downtown L.A.

Here, he married that girl he had given an engagement ring, but the two soon divorced. The split did not come before his ex-wife learned about Bonin's recurring dream, which would eventually set the stage for someone else's nightmares.

"He told me he had the dream a lot of times," said Susan Bonin. "He would be in a bar alone and he would walk up to a girl who had no face. He would buy her a drink and take her to a deserted place. There, he'd rape her, kill her and bury her in a shallow grave."

He would wake up in tears, she said.

Something triggers string of assaults

Whether it was post-traumatic stress disorder from serving in Vietnam – "You learn that life is cheap over there," he later told a radio station shortly before his scheduled execution - the end of his marriage or the subsequent return to his mother's home, Bonin could no longer contain his urges.

Playing a big role were likely the memories of how much he enjoyed having complete control over another person – as he did when he assaulted his fellow soldiers in Vietnam at gunpoint, having them completely at his mercy.

Shortly after moving back in with his mother, Bonin abducted and sexually assaulted four teenage boys – 14-year-old William, 17-year-old John, 12-year-old Larry and 18-year-old Jesus - forcing them to perform oral sex on him before sodomizing them and performing excruciating methods of torture that included squeezing their testicles.

When Bonin was finally apprehended in 1969, he was driving with a 16-year-old male passenger, and he told police officers that they were lucky that they had caught him because he felt that he might have killed the boy.

During evaluations before his trial, Bonin was diagnosed as a "mentally disordered sex offender amenable to treatment," and was placed under observation at Atascadero State Hospital in San Luis Obispo County.

Doctors then were able to determine through physical evidence including scars on his head and buttocks the levels of abuse Bonin had suffered as a child, despite his lack of memory regarding any incident. They also reported signs of manic depression, as well as damage to the area of the brain that restrains violent impulses.

Professionals worked with him for two years, but Bonin was unable to shake his lust for young men, and he ended up being discharged from the hospital in 1971 and sent to jail in to finish out his sentence after officials at the hospital ultimately found him untreatable.

"He wanted to straighten himself out, but doesn't know how to go about it," one expert wrote in a report that should have led to a lengthy sentence.

Still, his stint behind bars was horrifying in its brevity, and he was released in May of 1974 after doctors determined he was "no longer a danger to others."

It would be a terrible mistake, and it didn't take long before Bonin was back to his old sadistic tricks.

A wrong-way ride

About 16 months after his release from jail, Bonin ran into 14-year-old hitchhiker David McVicker, who was hitching a ride to his home in Huntington Beach.

It was the last day of summer in 1975.

"I was actually hitchhiking home from Garden Grove to Huntington Beach and he got me," said McVicker, who at first noticed nothing strange about the man in the blue Opel Cadet. "He was totally cool. There was nothing in the least bit strange about him."

At least not until Bonin asked McVicker if he was gay, and the young hitchhiker asked Bonin to stop the car. The driver then pulled out a gun.

"That's when I knew I was in trouble," McVicker said.

Bonin drove to a deserted field and brutally raped the teenager, then attempted to strangle him with his own T-shirt. When McVicker screamed, Bonin apologized and drove him home, where he ominously said, "We'll meet again."

As many rape victims will attest, McVicker's ordeal was hardly over.

His mother was reticent to talk about the details of the horrors her son had faced at the hands of a madman, so he had no one to talk to about his sorrow, rage and terror except for his best friend, who was too young to provide the support McVicker needed. For a boy who had been forced to grow up much too fast, the normalcy of school was nearly impossible to bear.

He eventually dropped out, but painful memories still followed. He endured listening to acquaintances make jokes at his expense, and lost a job after a boss read an article which suggested that McVicker had survived because he, too, was an accomplice, and fired him.

"It's like being raped again," he said.

Decades after the incident, he lives on disability because of the debilitating effects his rape and its aftermath had on his life.

He still has nightmares.

Back to prison

The assault on McVicker — along with another attempted abduction of a teen - led to another prison sentence for Bonin, although the one to 15 years sentence he received at the California Men's Facility in San Luis Obispo seems woefully inadequate for attempted murder, considering his string of previous sex crimes.

Authorities had promised McVicker that Bonin's sentence would be 15 years to life, which had given the teen peace of mind knowing that his rapist would be doing hard time for his crime.

But instead of doing serious time, Bonin was released on October 11, 1978 – after serving just three years - and was given 18 months of supervised probation.

"Our society surely has its priorities misplaced when someone with Bonin's record of contempt for the personal integrity of others is released in the blink of an eye, while dealers of controlled substances - even in relatively small quantities - are given 10-year, 20-year and life terms," Circuit Judge Alex Kozinski later wrote when denying one of Bonin's appeals.

He moved in with his mother in the old family home and landed a job as a truck driver with Dependable Driveaway in Montebello. He also began dating a girl. Friends said that he liked to take her roller skating every Sunday in nearby Anaheim.

Still, there was something evil hovering around in William Bonin, and it would take no time at all for it to come out.

His neighbor, Everett Fraser, regularly hosted parties at his house, and it was there that Bonin met 22-year-old factory worker Vernon Butts – an amateur magician who also dabbled in the occult - and 19-year-old Texas transplant Gregory Miley, who eventually became both a lover and an accomplice to murder.

"I had all kinds of people coming to my house all the time," Fraser said. "That's why he liked coming over to my place, because he knew he would meet a lot of young people through me."

According to experts, between 10 to 25 percent of all serial killers like to hunt in pairs, and Bonin apparently wanted someone else to enjoy the fun of the freeways of California. It was a landscape tailor made to suit his lust for young men, especially during the period when so many disenfranchised kids were looking for something more meaningful in their lives, and almost always expected to find it in sun-drenched California.

Within a short time, Bonin's olive-green van became an instrument of death, and his accomplices became witnesses to one man's descent into madness.

First murder reveals degree of depravity

While some serial killers begin with simple murders, then become desensitized to it all and escalate into more depraved behavior, William Bonin was depraved from the start.

And his first victim would show that Bonin liked them young and he found significant satisfaction in sadistic torture.

One accomplice later said that Bonin loved to hear them scream, that his victims' expressions of pain gave him the most sexual and visceral pleasure.

Thomas Glen Lundgren was 13 years old when he left his parents' home in Reseda on May 28, 1979. It was early, and he hitched a ride, unfortunately ending up in the back of Bonin's outfitted van, where he would become a temporary plaything for both Bonin and Butts.

The handles on the doors in the back of the van had been removed, so once inside, prisoners weren't going anywhere. A variety of different ligatures, knives and odds and ends were stashed within reach. Bonin had figured out everything.

The dark-haired boy was found later that day, his penis and testicles removed, his throat slashed, his body covered in stab wounds and showing signs of strangulation.

The vicious stabbing, one expert would later say, is common in murders committed by gay men who feel some sense of shame about their sexuality, and each new blow with a blade is seen as a futile attempt by the murderer to silence his own homosexual urges.

Bonin later said that Thomas was not one of his victims - "I don't cut the dicks off little boys," he told one reporter in a sharp, angry tone – and ultimately he wasn't tried for Lundgren's murder. Officially, authorities still link Bonin to Thomas Lundgren's murder.

A careless slip puts 20 boys in danger

That summer, Bonin was arrested for molesting a 17-year-old boy, and because he was on probation, he should have been immediately returned to prison to serve out the rest of his sentence. An administrative error led him to be released before his court date, and as for that, he just decided not to show.

His neighbor, Everett Fraser, picked Bonin up from the Orange County jail.

On the way home, Bonin told Fraser, "No one's going to testify again. This is never going to happen to me again."

It was late summer before Bonin and Butts struck again, this time picking up 17-year-old Mark Shelton, who was walking to a movie theater near Beach Boulevard.

As part of his torture, Mark was raped with various objects found in the back of the van, including a stick. The torture was apparently so brutal that his body went into shock and he died.

His killers tossed him in San Bernardino County, but because their victim had died before they had had enough fun, they were anything but satisfied with the kill.

They had destroyed Mark's family — his father, Don, was desperate for revenge when police told him his son was dead — but it wasn't enough for the two villains.

The next day, they again went hunting, while Mark's father's anger simmered and festered.

"I was consumed with rage," Shelton said. "One day I walked out into my garden, saw my scarecrow perched there, and demolished it with a shovel. I just bashed it to pieces. If that hadn't happened I might have done something worse later on."

Vacation becomes date with death

German exchange student Marcus Grabs was celebrating his 17th year with a backpacking tour of the United States, one last free-spirited adventure before adulthood officially set in. He was on his own, but met a wide variety of different people as he traveled, and enjoyed that as much as seeing the many diverse sights a different country had to offer.

Marcus was last spotted hitchhiking along the Pacific Coast Highway.

At some time during the evening of August 5, 1979, the 17-year-old was picked up by Bonin and Butts, and the back of Bonin's van – and later Bonin's house when his mother was not at home - became a nightmare of sodomy, beating and death.

After they were done with him, they tossed Marcus's naked, battered body into the Malibu Canyon. When his body was discovered the next day, he had suffered more than 70 stab wounds – again an attempt by Bonin to "kill" his homosexuality, experts said - had a yellow nylon rope around his neck and an electrical cord around one of his ankles.

His killer "was like a rabid dog that has gone insane and doesn't know when to stop biting," a homicide detective later said.

Brutality doesn't quell hunger

It didn't take long for Bonin's urges to kick in again.

On August 29, 1979, 15-year-old Donald Hyden Jr. – a blond boy with a toothy grin – was hanging out in Hollywood, walking around the busiest part of Los Angeles, where so many dreams are made, and so many dreams completely fail.

Born in Cincinnati, Donald found himself in California after his parents Donald and Mary divorced and Mary decided the move to the West Coast would be good for her, Donald and his younger brother and sister.

The divorce hit him hard, and without his father around for guidance, Donald got into some trouble. He ended up living with his grandparents for a while, where he played baseball and voraciously followed the career of his idol, Pete Rose.

Still, Donald wanted to be with his mother and siblings, so he moved to their apartment in Hollywood in 1977.

When he was picked up during the early hours of August 27, 1979, walking along the Santa Monica Boulevard, he likely never imagined that he would end up strangled and tossed into a trash bin near the Ventura Freeway, discarded like so much garbage.

Bonin and Butts had abducted the young man and tortured him throughout the night. His body was discovered at around 11 a.m., about 10 hours after he was last seen.

He had been stabbed in both the neck and genitals, he had burn marks and bruising and he, like Marcus, had been violated with a fist or something similar in size, as shown by the distention of his anus. Donald had also been hit in the head before being strangled and tossed away.

If Butts had any qualms about following Bonin's descent into hell, he didn't show it. In fact, he seemed to like the "good little nightmare" that he and his friend were inflicting on southern California.

"After the first one, I couldn't do anything about it," Butts later said about following Bonin's murderous lead. "He had a hypnotic way about him."

CHAPTER 2:
William Bonin was hungry

Less than two weeks after Donald Hyden Jr. found himself in the back of Bonin's van, on September 9, 1979, 17-year-old David Murillo was riding his bike near his home in La Mirada, on his way to the movie theater where he planned to bring the weekend to a close with a Sunday night movie. ("Apocalypse Now" was tops at the box office that weekend, alongside Monty Python's "Life of Brian.")

Bonin and Butts spotted him and lured him into the van, were he was bound, raped repeatedly and strangled. His head was bashed in with a tire iron for good measure.

His body was found three days later, lying alongside Highway 101.

Eight days later, 18-year-old Newport Beach resident Robert Wirostek was riding his bike to his job as a clerk at a grocery store.

He never made it to work, but his body was found on September 19, dumped alongside I-10.

There was a period of a few months when Bonin and his accomplice Butts laid low, but by November, they had a hunger that needed to be satisfied.

On the 29th of the month, just after Thanksgiving, Bonin and Butts abducted an unidentified teen, beating him, raping him and strangling him to death before dumping him in Kern County.

The next day, still on a high from the previous day's kill, Bonin and Butts struck again.

This time, it would be 17-year-old Frank Dennis Fox, 17, of Bellflower, who found himself in the back of the green van on November 30.

"He'd been home a few days earlier and I gave him some stuff for his apartment," said his mother, Jerri. "He wanted me to cut his hair."

He had been dumped on Ortega Highway, just five miles east of Interstate I-5.

His body showed signs of beating, and there were ligature marks on his ankles, wrists and neck. There were avocado green carpet fibers tangled in his pubic hair, and there were signs of sexual activity.

Later, at trial, those carpet fibers would prove to be an important bit of evidence.

The carpet in the back of Bonin's van featured the same swirled pattern featured on the fibers found clinging to Fox's hair. It was also avocado green.

Fox might not have survived his encounter with Bonin and Butts, but he would certainly do his part in death to see his killers brought to justice, even if it was from the grave.

A sick Christmas gift

As the Christmas holiday grew closer, Bonin again headed out on the weekend to hunt for a new victim. He trolled the freeways on Fridays and Saturdays, reserving Sundays for his girlfriend.

This time the unlucky teen would be 15-year-old John Kilpatrick, who left his mother's house to visit some friends and never returned. He had been wearing sandals and blue nylon shorts on the night he was last seen by those who loved him.

Because John often went away for days at a time – he was having trouble dealing with the divorce of his parents, and missed his father, who lived in Cincinnati – and friends had mistakenly reported seeing him at the mall, he wasn't reported missing until February.

"I didn't think he had run away," said his mother, Pricilla Kilpatrick. "We just thought he was thinking things out and we didn't want to scare him off."

She found out how wrong the reports of sightings were when a friend called her to say that her son – whose tattoos of a skull wearing a hat on his right bicep and an F on his right hand were the identifying marks she and authorities needed – was likely a victim of the Freeway killer.

"I knew it was him before the police even came out," she said. "I didn't want to believe it, but I knew it was him because of the tattoos. His brother had put them on him."

Kilpatrick – who was the sixth of seven children - was identified in August of 1980.

A grisly New Year's celebration

On January 1, 1980, Bonin rang in the new decade with a solo murder.

On this day, he brutalized and strangled a 16-year-old Rialto youth named Michael Francis McDonald.

His body was found fully clothed, disposed of in San Bernardino County, but he wasn't identified until March 24, a day that would play a critical role in the capture of Bonin.

For a while, Bonin was satiated, but a month later, he again felt the need to kill.

This time, 15-year-old Charles Miranda disappeared while looking for a little fun in a busy section of Hollywood.

Bonin had with him a new assistant, Gregory Matthews Miley, on Feb. 3, 1980, when they ran across Charles, who was hitchhiking along the Santa Monica Boulevard.

At first, the young man with thick brown hair only had to give up the $6 he had stashed in his wallet, but soon enough the two had overpowered him and tied him up so Bonin could have his way with him.

Miley attempted to rape Miranda as well, but was unable to sustain an erection, so he used sharp objects he found in the back of the van instead, brutally assaulting Charles to hide his embarrassment.

Bonin said to Miley, "Kid's going to die. Kid's going to - this kid's going to die," to which Miley replied, "Why don't you just let the kid go?"

Bonin refused, and said, "No, because he'll know us and he'll know the van."

He then demonstrated his preferred method of murder for Miley.

"Can you do it?" Bonin asked Miley as he began choking the boy. "Let me show you how to do this."

Bonin then strangled Charles, using a tire iron to twist the shirt like a tourniquet, while Miley, apparently enjoying his first kill a bit too much, jumped repeatedly on Charles' chest.

They dumped his naked body in an alleyway in downtown Los Angeles, then disposed of his clothing and other items. Bonin then turned to Miley and said, "I'm horny, let's go and do another one."

Miley at first protested, and said, "Oh, man, no way. I don't want to do it no more. I just want to go home," but eventually helped find Bonin's next victim.

The unluckiest boy on earth

The unlucky victim would be 12-year-old James Macabe, who was waiting at a Huntington Beach bus stop for a ride to Disneyland.

He'd been staying with his older brother while his parents were away for the weekend, and he'd been dropped off at the bus stop by his brother, who had also given him money for admission.

According to Miley, James got into the van willingly, likely too distracted with the idea of roller coasters and Mickey Mouse to recognize the danger of taking a ride with strangers.

And instead of heading to the happiest place on earth, James had entered hell, and Bonin parked in a grocery store parking lot and got in the back of the van, where he repeatedly raped and beat the 12-year-old boy as he cried.

Miley listened in for a while, then joined Bonin in the abuse because he "felt like it." Bonin then strangled James with his T-shirt, again using the tire iron for leverage.

James' body was found three days later, on February 6, 1980, alongside a dumpster.

Bonin later told reporter David Lopez of KNXT-TV that of the 21 boys and young men that he is believed to have killed, "that little kid was the easiest one to kill."

His mother never recovered, and 16 years after her son's death, she was still looking for ways to keep the loss of her son off her mind.

"You know that country song "'No Future in the Past?'" said Anna Macabe, in reference to the Vince Gill title. "There isn't."

About a month later, on March 14, 1980, 18-year-old Ronald Gatlin disappeared from North Hollywood. His body was found the next day, dead from strangulation, with ligature marks on his ankle, wrist and neck, evidence of sexual activity before his death along with evidence of beating.

The body count was starting to pile up in southern California.

Close call leads to new 'friend'

On one particular night, Bonin was hanging out at his neighbor Everett Fraser's place, and decided to leave about the same time as 17-year-old William Pugh. Bonin offered the teen a ride, and on the way to Pugh's house, he asked the young man who was still wearing braces if he wanted to have sex.

The question caused the teen to want more than anything a way out of the vehicle, and he attempted to escape when Bonin slowed for a stoplight.

The killer responded by grabbing Pugh by the collar and dragging him back into the passenger seat. He then told Pugh about his favorite weekend activities, and talked about how much he enjoyed "picking up" young male hitchhikers for sex, torture and murder.

Bonin then said, "If you want to kill somebody, you should make a plan and find a place to dump the body before you even pick a victim," before dropping him Pugh off at his house unharmed.

Pugh becomes Bonin's latest accomplice

After having survived a night with William Bonin, Pugh was apparently intrigued by the idea of rape and murder, and instead of going to police, on March 20, the teen with a long rap sheet filled with various petty crimes joined Bonin in the abduction of Harry Todd Turner, a 15-year-old runaway who had escaped a boys' group home and was working on getting as far away from the place as possible.

According to Pugh, he and Bonin lured Harry into the van by offering him $20 for sex.

The boy was agreeable, but it wouldn't be the kind of sex he was expecting.

After Bonin tied up the teen, he brutally raped him, then bit him on the genitals hard enough to draw blood and ordered Pugh to "beat him up."

Pugh did as he was told, and bludgeoned the boy into submission.

Bonin then strangled Harry with his T-shirt using the tire iron as a tool before they tossed his body into a Los Angeles alleyway. Bite marks were clearly evident on his penis, as were signs of a savage sexual assault.

An autopsy later determined that his skull had been fractured in eight places.

Kills become big, big thrills

On March 22, 1980, police found the bodies of two boys alongside Ortega Highway in the Cleveland National Forest, 14-year-old Glen Norman Barker, who was spotted hitchhiking after telling his mother he had plans to stay with a friend, and 15-year-old Russell Duane Rugh, a student at Westminster High School who was last seen at a bus stop waiting to catch a ride to his job at a nearby fast food joint.

Both boys were naked and their bodies had bruises from being beaten. Both had ligature marks on their wrists and ankles as well as around their necks.

Both had been raped, but again, there were carpet fibers clinging to their pubic hair, allowing them to speak from the grave.

In a vicious new twist, Glen had a serious of cigarette burns looping around his neck.

Glen's mother, Sharon Barker, had been diagnosed with cervical cancer that had been treated into remission when she found out that her son was dead.

Making the news so much worse was the knowledge that she had warned her son about taking rides from strangers, and had given him bus money to visit his friend so he wouldn't have to put himself in danger.

But Glen had spent his bus money, and was forced to hitch a ride.

"He was not supposed to get in the van with anyone," said his grandfather, Elza Rodgers. "But you know how these boys are."

The news devastated his mother, Rodgers said, and significantly impacted her already fragile health.

"It didn't help her very much with the cancer," said Rodgers. "It really was a strain on her."

Still, the divorced mom did what she could to manage her job at Kmart, which she later juggled as best she could during Bonin's murder trial, which she attended religiously to both represent and remember her son.

Unfortunately, she was unable to see the boy's killer brought to justice.

Barker died three years after Bonin's conviction, while he was still sitting on death row, and where he would sit for 14 more years.

"She told me she would like to have lived to see Bonin die. It was the only regret she had," said Rodgers. "She really hated him."

Bodies of boys pile up

Despite the distinct, unwavering similarities in many of the murder victims, police were still unwilling to make an official call regarding a serial killer hunting down young boys throughout Los Angeles and Orange counties.

It was just as well, because there were two other killers making the rounds in southern California, and eventually, all of them would become known as the Freeway Killer.

CHAPTER 3:
Orange County Register unearths Bonin's secrets

Reporter J.J. Maloney remembers covering the story of the Freeway Killer for the Orange County Register.

The paper had run a story in 1979 about the bodies of boys turning up, strangled and violated, but no other media picked up on it, and the police were still unsure about a connection.

The story idled until Maloney ran across an envelope of clippings labeled "Dead Gay Boys," and felt compelled to follow the leads in that envelope, including the story of 12-year-old James McCabe, snatched on his way to Disneyland – "a little boy who'd wanted to see Donald Duck and Mickey Mouse, and instead ended up in an envelope labeled 'Dead Gay Boys," Maloney recalled.

Given the details in the folder, Maloney felt sure that it was the work of a serial killer, and he encouraged his editor to assign him to the story.

He played upon the man's emotions as a father in order to get the gig.

"It appeared certain that a psychopathic killer was on the loose, and that kind of killer, once he starts, repeats and repeats and repeats," Maloney wrote, years afterward. "One killer, one spree. If the police wouldn't say it publicly, someone had to."

The police weren't interested in serial killer theories, and told Maloney that it wasn't such a rarity to find so many strangled young men in the area, given the large gay population.

"The police naturally do not want the massive public pressure a serial killer brings to bear on them. And there are differences of opinion among policemen on the wisdom of giving out information to the public," Maloney wrote. "At the Register we felt the public had a right to know - that, more importantly, hitchhikers had a right to know that the next time they stuck their thumb out they might end up strangled and abused."

A profile of murder

Dr. Albert Rosenstein, a forensic psychologist whose opinion was enlisted by the Orange County Register, profiled the killer before Bonin was zeroed in on by police. He was chillingly accurate.

"The guy who's doing these murders is crazy," Rosenstein said. "The chance that he's been a mental patient at one time or another is very high. And the only place in Southern California where mentally disturbed sex offenders are sent is Patton

State Hospital." (The hospital where Bonin was housed was a bit north, so it was off of Rosenstein's radar.)

"The killer is a strong, clever white man in his late 20s or early 30s. If he were not strong, he could not handle the bodies. If he were not clever, he would have been caught already. If he were not white, he could not have picked up so many white youths. If he were not in his 20s or 30s, he would not be this kind of murdering sex offender, past studies have shown," Rosenstein said, also zeroing in on Bonin's sexual trauma as a child.

"As a result of some traumatic sexual experience as a child, the killer has developed into a bisexual, but he never has become comfortable with the homosexual side of his personality," he said. "He cruises the streets in a van, looking for young, white hitchhikers. He picks them up and offers them a drink, an alcoholic beverage laced with a drug. Once his victims are drugged, he assaults them sexually in the back of the van. After he's done that, he finds what he's done so repugnant that he feels he has to commit acts of sexual mutilation on their bodies after he has killed them."

The only thing Rosenstein got wrong was the sheer pleasure Bonin took in killing his victims. Rather than revulsion, he enjoyed the screams, the begging for mercy, the pain he inflicted, and reveled in his control over the boys who were unfortunate enough to get into his van.

"Bonin loved the killing," said Orange County prosecutor Sterling E. Norris. "He delighted in talking about it."

The story breaks

And on March 24, 1980, "We broke the story that a serial killer was at work in Southern California. We called him the 'Freeway Killer,'" Maloney said.

Even then, with so many similar murders, so many details linking the crimes, many officers believed that the Freeway Killer was little more than a story crafted by journalists to sell papers.

"I believe it was The Orange County Register that started all this," said Captain Walt Ownbey of the Los Angeles County Sheriff's Department. "This has built up and created a lot of fear about a killer or group of killers, and there is no evidence substantiating any of that."

It was, he said, "a total figment in the minds of journalists."

Still, police did have a team investigating potential links between a handful of cases.

"We're monitoring five cases since May of 1979 for any link among the five as well as 18 we've heard about in the multijurisdictional (southern California) area," Ownbey said. "But I must emphasize we don't have any evidence linking them. In this county alone, we have 35 to 40 dumps alone.

"It's not unusual to find similarities in five dumps a year, young boys, old men or young women," said the captain, who clearly had become jaded by the number of murder cases his office handled each year. "And you have to remember that 90 percent of all murders are done in only four ways: you shoot them, stab them, strangle them or blunt-force them."

He blamed the desire to pin the murders on a single killer to a growing exposure to serial killers.

"People are more inclined – due to the recent history of multiple murderers like Son of Sam, Hillside Strangler and the Trash Bag Murders – to read things into them. Maybe it's a sign of the times."

Still, the Orange County Register stuck to the story like glue, and soon enough, television stations also picked up the Freeway Killer story and ran with it.

"The freeway plays such an important part because it's so easy to get away," said CBS reporter David Lopez. "You could drive forever on those freeway exchanges."

With so much media attention – along with a reward for information about the killer – schools began warning students about the dangers of hitchhiking and tips began coming in, both to the newspaper and the Orange and Los Angeles County police departments.

"There were more bodies and more bodies," Lopez said. "Then in late 1979, you realized there was a mass murderer out there."

So many bodies were found, said Earle Robitaille, who was then police chief of Huntington Beach, that "it was no longer 'Is it going to happen again?' but 'who's going to be the next victim, and where will he be abducted and where will he be picked up?'"

"He was so systematic and predictable," Robitaille said. "That was the scary part."

CHAPTER 4:
Bonin's trail of death, torture continues

On April 11, 1980, the nude body of 16-year-old Steven Wood was found in an alley in Long Beach near the Pacific Coast Highway.

He had been on his way to school after a trip to the dentist when he encountered Bonin.

The last thing he had said to his mother was, "See you later, alligator." Of course she responded, "After a while, crocodile."

When he was found, his body showed signs of beating about the face and elsewhere and there were ligature marks on at least one ankle and wrist as well as on his neck.

Steven's murder devastated the entire family, which virtually imploded after his death.

"I live in a different world now," said Steven's mother, Barbara Biehn, in an interview with the Los Angeles Times. "There's just too much to remember."

Her son Carl, 20 when his brother's body was found on April 11, had a particularly hard time accepting his brother's murder.

"He just went off the deep end," said Biehn, adding that on Bonin's birthday, January 8, 1989, he rode his bike to a local discount store to purchase a shotgun and ammunition. He then pedaled to a friend's house, and shot himself to death in the garage.

"He was hurting for nine years," she said of Carl, who tried to suppress his pain with drugs, then sank deep into an addiction that brought signs of mental illness into the light. "It was an absolute nightmare at the end."

Their family blown apart, Biehn and her husband moved to Arizona to escape the daily reminders of their sons – their schools, their friends, their favorite hangouts - but they still carry with them the demons that are memories, and they stick to themselves now, avoiding making any new friends.

"They're happy. They have good things going on," she said of the people she doesn't want to know. "And I don't think we do."

Torture methods escalate

On April 29, 1980, Darin Lee Kendrick, 19, was collecting carts in the parking lot at the grocery store where he worked when

Bonin and Butts enticed him into the van with the promise of drugs.

When his naked body was found the next day, it revealed the nightmare Kendrick had suffered during his time with Bonin and Butts.

He had been brutally sodomized and beaten, and had also been restrained, as shown by the ligature marks on one ankle and wrist as well as around his neck.

He had a stab wound to the top of his spinal cord thanks to the ice pick that had been lodged in his ear and he had chemical burns on his mouth, chin, chest and stomach from being forced to drink hydrochloric acid.

Earl Hanson, an attorney who represented Bonin during his confession, said the need for more violence was similar to the escalating need of a drug addict.

"He had to constantly increase the dosage to get the same euphoria," Hanson said.

CHAPTER 5:
A consummate serial killer

In the same way that William Bonin's actions fit the pattern of most serial killers – he waited until his need to kill was overwhelming, then he acted on those desired and was satiated – his past also helped set the course for future events.

And many said that William Bonin never really had a chance.

"He was faced with so many significant hurdles when he was young that made it virtually impossible for him to be a successful human being," said one of his public defenders just hours before his execution.

According to Heather Mitchell and Michael G. Aamodt of Virginia's Radford University, Radford University, the majority of serial killers suffered physical abuse, sexual abuse, psychological abuse or neglect as children.

One expert, Robert K. Ressler, considered the foremost authority on serial killers – he coined the term – went so far as to say "100 percent had been abused as children, either with violence, neglect or humiliation."

For Bonin, his parents were drunks who ended up abandoning him at his grandfather's house, knowing that the man was a pedophile. After staring down that nightmare, Bonin acted out, only to find himself in a detention center at age 8, surrounded by much older, equally troubled kids who continued the sexual abuse.

With those unexplained scars, it was clear that he'd suffered significant physical abuse as well.

In terms of what makes a serial killer, Bonin's past was a horrible trifecta of abuse, neglect and brain damage that impacted his ability to exact rational control.

"Normal parents? Normal brains? I think not," said Dr. Jonathan Pincus, a neurologist and author of the book "Base Instincts: What Makes Killers Kill."

"Abusive experiences, mental illnesses and neurological deficits interplayed to produce the tragedies reported in the newspapers. The most vicious criminals have also been, overwhelmingly, people who have been grotesquely abused as children and have paranoid patterns of thinking," said Pincus in his book, adding that childhood traumas can impact the developmental anatomy and functioning of the brain.

And although Bonin suppressed his memories of his abuse, doctors pointed to the scars and the damage to the frontal lobe of his brain as unimpeachable evidence.

"There is much data to indicate that Bonin was severely and recurrently sexually abused as a child," said one psychiatrist.

Bonin knows no boundaries

During Bonin's year of living dangerously, he sometimes was perfectly capable of living a semi-normal life during the hours when he was not hunting for boys.

While his girlfriend was long gone, he did have a new lover, Lawrence Eugene Sharp, an 18-year-old from Long Beach that Bonin once took to Knott's Berry Farm, a California theme park, for a date.

Unfortunately for Lawrence, Bonin grew tired of his lovers as quickly as he did with his victims, and at some point between April 10 and May 18 of 1980, Bonin killed him, stuffing his body in a trash bin behind a gas station.

"I just got up one morning and decided I was tired of him," Bonin said when asked why he chose to kill his teenage lover. "I just got tired of having him around and so I decided that I should kill him."

Bonin later told the TV reporter David Lopez that if he had not been arrested, "I'd still be killing. I couldn't stop killing. It got easier with each victim I did."

A solo killing leaves victim's family in turmoil

On May 19, Bonin wanted Vernon Butts to go with him on a hunting trip, but Butts said no. In a rare murder on his own, Bonin abducted 14-year-old Sean King, who was hanging around a Downey bus stop, tortured him, raped him, strangled him and discarded his body. He then went back to brag about it to Butts.

Initially, King's body wasn't found, and the boy's mother Lavada Gifford, allegedly wrote Bonin an impassioned plea to tell police where her son's body was so she could bury him by Christmas. But it wasn't her letter that caused the heartless Bonin to give up the information. It was a craving for a burger.

"I was dying for a hamburger and I knew if I went out with the cops they would buy me a hamburger," Bonin told reporter David Lopez.

In exchange, he would not be tried for Sean King's murder at trial.

Later, with Bonin behind bars awaiting his date with the executioner, Gifford wrote a flurry of letters to her son's killer in hopes of hearing from him some element of remorse.

"I saw on TV in 1989 that Bonin had become a born-again Christian, and I needed to know if he had made any real peace with his Lord and had any remorse," she said. "He wrote me back more than 13 times, but did he ever say he was sorry? Not one word. It was all about him and his favorite TV shows.

He never acknowledged that he did anything wrong. So I stopped."

Homeless man becomes Bonin's new roommate – and accomplice

Nine days after Bonin dumped Sean King's body, he invited a 19-year-old drifter named James Munro to move into the 1950s tract house he shared with his mother.

The Michigan native happily accepted, and later said his initial impression of Bonin was that he was "a good guy, really normal."

That reputation continued after Bonin also helped Munro land a job at Dependable Driveaway in Montebello, the same place Bonin himself worked.

Story doesn't bypass Bonin's attention

In an effort to keep an eye on whether or not police were honing in on him and his van of death, Bonin drove daily to Orange County to purchase the Register, and it was the March 24, 1980, story – the one that broke the news of a serial killer targeting southern California's boys – that sealed his fate.

To those who weren't his accomplices, Bonin seemed obsessed with the story, and collected clippings on the Freeway Killer that he stored in a scrapbook he kept in his van.

"Bill'd bring in the newspaper, and say, 'This guy got another one.' And I'd say, 'Damn it Bill, I wish they'd catch this guy. It's guys like this that give other good gay guys a bad name," said Everett Fraser, his longtime friend and neighbor.

The Register had included a photo of a suspicious van linked to the dead bodies – it was a drawing, but included every detail but Bonin's "C.B. Trucker" sticker in the back window - and their disappearances.

For that first story, the Register had also included photos of many of the strangling victims, and Bonin pointed them out to one of his accomplices, and told him that he was the madman rounding up the young men.

"He said, 'Well, this is No. 7, or 14, or 12,'" the accomplice later said in court.

The police finally recognized the pattern associated with many of Bonin's victims, and departments throughout the region began working together in hopes of capturing the Freeway Killer.

"There was total paranoia in the community, particularly there near the end," said Earle Robitaille, whose Huntington Beach paradise was one of Bonin's favorite hunting grounds. "It was a very tough time."

Orange County investigator Bernie Esposito was also on edge.

"You went home at the end of the day and held your breath that the damned phone didn't ring with another one," Esposito said, adding that the string of murders was unforgettable.

"Some of them were stabbed, most of them were strangled, but the thing that stands out in my mind is the pain he inflicted on these boys and the callous disregard he had for them," the detective said. "He treated them as a sex object that was just there for his gratification. I looked across the breakfast table at my 14-year-old son and I just imagined how I would feel if police came knocking at my door in the middle of the night and told me that my son had been brutally murdered and left in some field like a bag of trash."

Esposito and his partner formed a task force with four other officers – two from LAPD and two from Los Angeles County - and they made it their mission to track down the person responsible for the body count, which was quickly escalating.

"At the start of 1980, there were bodies coming in every two weeks," recalled investigator Jim Sidebotham. "Long Beach was getting them, L.A. was getting them like crazy. San Bernardino was getting them. Riverside was getting them."

Then rape victim David McVicker – who was almost strangled with a T-shirt and a tire iron in Bonin's signature method - recognized something in the assaults of the dead men that looked familiar, and called cops to tell them he was fairly sure he knew who the Freeway Killer was.

"I kept reading the newspapers, and every time I would read these stories about these kids coming up dead, it was like just in my stomach. I could just feel this," McVicker told Nancy Grace. "I knew what they went through. And then after a year of that, it was just kind of overwhelming to me. I finally called the sheriff's department and said, 'He's supposed to be locked up, but he's not.' I didn't know. They needed to find out where he was. And as it was, he was killing everybody."

He ended up talking to Esposito, who recalled vividly the story he heard.

"McVicker tells me that after Bonin had done everything he wanted to do with him, he said, 'you know what, you're an alright guy. I was going to kill you but I want to come back for you and use you again,'" Esposito recalled.

It sent chills down his spine.

A second tip came when 17-year-old William Pugh was arrested for car theft.

Pugh, who had been along for the ride the night Bonin killed Harry Todd Turner, told police he had some information he would share about the Freeway Killer if they would make a deal in the car theft. He failed to mention his role in the murder of Henry Todd Turner, but he did tell police that a guy he knew, William Bonin, had a glove box full of newspaper clippings about the case.

An investigation into Bonin's background revealed a string of convictions for assaulting teenage boys, including David McVicker.

Detectives made a stop at Everett Fraser's house for some background, although it wasn't until they showed him a map that detailed his house, Bonin's house, the place where one victim had disappeared and the location of Bonin's favorite liquor store as well as its proximity to the site of the disappearance that Fraser was convinced his friend was the killer.

"It just clicked. Something just clicked," Fraser said. "I said, 'Okay, get out your pencils, you guys. Get out your pads of paper.' They just looked at each other."

"The hair on his arm actually stood up," said detective Kirk Mellecker. "You could just see the entire switch in his viewpoint, once it dawned on him."

Now, with 33-year-old Bonin in their sights, police began trailing the serial killer, waiting for him to make a move.

The last victim

It was early on June 2, 1980, when Bonin and a drifter names James Munro spotted Steven Wells along the freeway.

The 19-year-old agreed to accompany the two back to their house for sex. They took Wells back to the house the devilish duo shared with Bonin's mother.

After an initial round of sex, Bonin offered Steven $200 if he could tie him up, and Steven – thinking little about the missing boys and men before him who had ended up as only a handful of paragraphs in a newspaper – agreed. Almost immediately, Bonin began to assault him, raping him ruthlessly as he struggled, helplessly bound.

Munro said he watched TV in another room until Bonin called for him.

"At that point I knew it was real. Bonin went to get a glass of water and I told him, 'No, don't do this.' But Bonin said, 'It's too late. There is nothing that you or I can do to stop it.'"

Later, Bonin showed little emotion as he described the murder.

"Both me and Jim beat him up prior to killing him," Bonin told police. "He said he wouldn't tell anyone, just to let him go. When we finally got around to killing him, we put a shirt around his neck. I twisted it, and he was strangled."

And while Bonin might have been calm in describing the murder, as it was happening, he was anything but.

Munro later recounted the events of that day to police, and recalled Bonin screaming at the equally hysterical Steven, "Shut up! You're going to die. It was like he was a monster."

Later, Bonin and Munro loaded the body into the van and went to visit Vernon Butts.

"As we went up to the door we knocked, and Butts came out dressed in a Darth Vadar uniform like the 'Star Wars' movie," Munro recalled. "We went inside, and Bonin told Butts, 'This is Jim Munro and he is my new partner.' Butts said, 'Hi,' and showed me all the people he killed. He showed me a closet containing 21 ID cards of all the victims that he killed. Bonin then told Butts to come look at what we did. So we all went out to the van. Bonin uncovered the body, and Butts replied, 'Oh how nice. You got another one.' Then Bonin asked Butts, 'Hey do you want to come with us, or do you want to stay here and watch the news?' Butts told Bonin that he would stay at the house. Bonin told Butts if he saw anything on the news to call him."

After leaving Butts' home, Munro helped Bonin dispose of Wells' body behind an abandoned gas station in Huntington Beach.

"We pulled into a closed Mobil gas station, dumped the body behind the gas station, and then took off," Munro said. "Then we went on our way home. As we were driving home - we stopped off at McDonald's, went to the drive thru window, and got some hamburgers. When we got home, we sat down. Bonin was eating a burger, looked up in the sky and said, 'Thanks Steve,' then looked down and said, 'Thanks Steve,' then looked at me and said, 'Where ever you are at,' and started to laugh."

'I'll kill you if you run'

Later that night, Bonin told Munro he'd better keep his mouth shut about the murder.

"Bonin told me that he was the 'Freeway Killer,' that he had other partners out there who helped him kill, and that he killed 45 people. I got scared, and started to cry again. He came up to me and told me to stop crying because he was not going to hurt me unless I ran, or called the police.

"Then he told me he was getting tired and wanted to go to bed. We went into his bedroom and he got into his bed, and I got into mine. Then he turned off the lights. I got up and turned the lights back on, and he asked me what was the matter. I told him I did not trust him, and I did not want him to kill me. He got up, came over to me, and told me, 'I know a way you can trust me.' I asked him, 'How?' He said, 'Let me tie you up. So you will know that I will not kill you.' I let him tie me up the same way that he tied up Wells. Then he told me that he could kill me, and that there was nothing I could do. I started to cry, and I pleaded for my life like Wells did.

"He started to laugh, and told me that he was not going to kill me. But if I ever ran from him he would kill me, and that if he could not get me - his partners would. I told him okay, and that I would not run. So he untied me. I was so scared. I did not want Bonin, or his partners, to get me. I could not believe what I had gotten myself into. It was like a murder movie. Like

'Friday the 13th,' and this time it was for real. I could not get it out of my mind. I wanted it to all end, but I did not know how. I stayed low for a while until June 13, 1980, when I heard that Bonin was arrested for murder."

Munro has since asked Wells' parents – who have made it their mission to keep Munro behind bars at every parole hearing – for forgiveness, and says he lives with many regrets.

"I was just a stupid kid. If I'd known that 15 years to life meant I was never going to get out of prison, I would never have pleaded guilty," Munro said in an interview with the Los Angeles Times. "Hooking up with Bonin was a huge mistake."

An unfortunate miss

If Bonin had spent a little more time savoring his time with Steven Wells, who would ultimately be his last murder victim, the man might have survived his nightmarish ordeal.

Police surveillance of William Bonin began June 2, 1980, the same night that Steven was killed.

But Steven was already dead, and just before police arrived to set up round-the-clock surveillance on Bonin, his tortured body had been carried out of the house in a cardboard box and callously dumped behind a service station.

"If it had gone down just a little bit earlier, we might have stopped" them, Sterling Norris said.

As it was, they finally had their eye on their suspect, and they were ready for him to make a move.

For about a week, William Bonin behaved just like any other single guy living in California.

He went to work as a truck driver each day, then hung out with friends including Fraser in the evenings before heading home for the night.

"I saw him about three times a week. I knew he was going out about every night, just like any other young guy, cruising," Fraser said. "He was always trying to get me to go out with him at night, but I never would. I always had to be at home."

Capture and confession

Laying low was smart, but nine days after Stephen Wells was killed, Bonin's demons were again hungry, and he began hunting for a new victim, completely oblivious to the police in his rear view because he was so focused on his mission.

He tried to pick up five different young men, police on his van's tail the entire time, until he finally succeeded with a 15-year-old boy.

Bonin drove his new prey to a deserted beach parking lot, and by the time police reached the van, they could hear disturbing sounds coming from inside.

Bonin was already in the process of raping and strangling his victim.

"The police almost waited too long, this kid was in the throes of being strangled in the back of that van," Lopez said.

Evidence connected to a slew of murders including tape and rope were found in the back of the van. Police also found Bonin's scrapbook of Freeway Killer stories, which made it even easier to determine which victims had been the work of William Bonin.

It was the night of June 11, 1980, and Bonin was booked on suspicion of murder and various sex charges.

He was held in lieu of $250,000 bond, and confessed to police that he had killed 21 boys and young men, who he then essentially "threw away like garbage."

Tricked into talking

He didn't confess willingly, however.

It wasn't until he read that letter from a woman whose son was still missing but presumed to be a victim of Bonin's that the man cracked.

He led authorities to the body of Sean King – although he later said he did it not to ease the mother's pain, but for the hamburger he knew officers would buy him for lunch – then told them everything about the 21 murders.

Later, "Jigsaw John" St. John, one of the officers whose work helped put not only Bonin but also his accomplices behind bars, pulled Los Angeles Deputy District Norris aside.

"I've got to tell you something," the detective said. "It wasn't Mrs. King who wrote the letter. It was me."

An encounter with the devil

As he confessed over the course of several evenings, Bonin casually told police the increasingly more grisly details of his murder spree.

"I tied him up with nylon - this electrician type of wire. I pulled a knife on him and he got scared. I stabbed him in the left arm. It surprised me that I did it," Bonin told police, recounting the murder of one of his victims. "I stabbed him again and then again, and again and again until he was helpless."

There were so many stab wounds because Bonin wasn't methodical or ritualistic about the stabbing, despite the intimacy of the torture.

"They would try to stop me from stabbing them and I would stab just to stab," Bonin said. "I stuck them in different places with the knife because I didn't know where to stab, you know I didn't know where any vital organs are or anything like that."

Those who heard his confession were horrified not only by the details of each of the murders, but also the casual way in which Bonin told them.

"The thing that struck me was he was sitting there telling us in graphic detail about how he brutalized, sexually abused and murdered these young boys like he's talking about yesterday's news," Esposito.

Bonin's lack of emotion or compassion "was just incredible," he recalled.

"There was not a policeman in that room who did not want to kill Bonin - to hear him talk about those kids," added Esposito's partner, Orange County investigator Jim Sidebotham. "You're in there trying to hold in your puke and to do your job."

It didn't help that the more Bonin talked, the more excited he became as he recalled victim after victim.

"This guy was impassioned about what he did. He loved it," said Norris, the district attorney who would eventually prosecute Bonin for his Los Angeles County crimes. "Listening to his confession was like sitting in a room of horrors. Here we are talking about killing kids, killing one and throwing him out like a piece of trash, and then going back to get another. It made me sick."

After police hear his confession, Bonin was formally charged with 14 counts of murder, eleven counts of robbery, plus one count each of sodomy and mayhem between July 26 and 29.

He also gave up his accomplices, who were by now scattered across the country.

Bonin's victims

The victim list is believed to be as follows:

1. Thomas Lundgren, 13 – May 28, 1979
2. Mark Shelton, 17 – August 4, 1979
3. Markus Grabs, 17 – August 5, 1979
4. Donald Hyden, 15 – August 27, 1979
5. David Murillo, 17 – September 9, 1979
6. Robert Wirostek, 18 – September 17, 1979
7. John Doe, believed to be 19-25 – November 29, 1979
8. Frank Dennis Fox, 17 – November 30, 1979
9. John Kilpatrick, 15 – December 10, 1979
10. Michael McDonald, 16 – January 1, 1980
11. Charles Miranda, 15 – February 3, 1980
12. James Macabe, 12 – February 3, 1980
13. Ronald Gatlin, 18 – March 14, 1980
14. Glenn Barker, 14 – March 21, 1980
15. Russell Rugh, 15 – March 21, 1980
16. Harry Todd Turner, 15 – March 24, 1980
17. Steven Wood, 16 – April 10, 1980
18. Lawrence Sharp, 18 – April 10, 1980
19. Darin Lee Kendrick, 19 – April 29, 1980
20. Sean King, 14 – May 19, 1980
21. Steven Wells, 18 – June 2, 1980

While these are the young men and boys that Bonin initially confessed to killing – he later disputed the murder of Thomas Lundgren, and told a reporter with a degree of indignation, "I do not cut the dicks off little boys." While the other boys were significantly tortured, Lundgren was the only one to be emasculated.

There are believed to be at least 20 other victims linked to Bonin, maybe more.

Of course, that's not to mention the families forced to live on knowing the horror of what happened to their child at the hands of William Bonin.

Losing a child sparks a degree of emotional pain that trumps the death of a parent or spouse – this is a person they raised and nurtured, and all the hopes and dreams they had for them have now been buried. Losing that child to homicide only accentuates that grief.

Experts say that depression, anxiety, rage, survivor guilt, blame, post-traumatic stress disorder and a desire for revenge are common for the parents who are forced to survive a life without their child because someone else deemed them not worthy to life.

The grief can be so overwhelming, some experts say, that it can reduce a parent's lifespan due to the damaging physical effects of stress and depression.

Taking them into consideration, Bonin's victim list rises considerably.

Butts lands behind bars

Police picked up 22-year-old Vernon Butts on July 25 after executing a search warrant and finding evidence of at least one of the killings in his Downey home.

Butts told police that he had had a limited role in the killings, and only held victims down for Bonin to rape and torture, although he admitted that he once used a coat hanger to torture one of their victims.

"We took him out the middle of nowhere and had sex with him, and then he killed him," Butts said.

He went along, Butts said, because Bonin was a Svengali of sorts and had a "hypnotic" effect on him, something that many other accomplices to serial killers have said about the men who have led them to commit heinous crimes.

"After the first one, I couldn't do anything about it," Butts said, adding that his murder spree with Bonin was "a good little nightmare."

He told police that Bonin bound his victims, leaving them completely defenseless. He would then beat them and have anal and oral sex with them before taking their lives.

When one of the boys resisted, Bonin "beat him up real bad," Butts said.

And while witnesses for the defense would later say that Bonin was ashamed of what he had done, the demented killer in fact took immense pleasure in snuffing the lives out of his victims, Butts said.

"He loved every minute of it, I guess," he added. "He loved to hear them scream, basically."

In his confession, Butts described the knives, ice picks and acid used in six of the murders.

He was charged as an accomplice in nine of the murders linked to Bonin.

Second accomplice arrested

About a month after Butts was behind bars, James Munro – who stole Bonin's car after he was arrested and fled the state - was tracked to Michigan, where state police arrested him as well.

"It was June 13, 1980, when Bonin was arrested. I was shocked, and it made me panic because I did not want to also be arrested. I waited until June 17 to talk to the cops - to see if I was also wanted for this crime. I came in the morning and talked to a cop. He asked me if I went around cruising with Bonin picking up hitchhikers," Munro said. "I told him, 'No! I don't know anything.' He told me that I could go for now. That night I took off, and I headed for Michigan.

"I stalled the cops for as long as I could - until I got busted for the murder of Steven Wells. That is when my nightmare began, and I would never wake up," he said.

"I was eating a sandwich when I heard a knock on the door," Munro said. "My cousin, Cindy, opened the door and the police came in. There were cops everywhere. It looked like the president of the United States was here. The cop that had a clipboard asked Cindy her name. Then he asked Jeff his name. Then he asked me my name. Then as he was leaving he looked at the report, and I matched the description that Bonin gave to the cops. So they got me, and took me outside. As I went outside there were reporters, TV cameras, and cops everywhere. They had taped off the entire area, and hundreds of people were watching - as I was being led off by the Michigan State Police and the Detectives of Michigan. When I got in the car my cousin asked me in shock, 'What the hell did you do?' I looked at her and I told her, 'I didn't do anything.' She just shook her head in disbelief, and in shock."

Munro's parents learned about his arrest on the evening news.

One of the arresting officers, Michigan State Police Trooper James Dowling, was already familiar with Munro, and called him "a regular, run of the mill pain in the neck."

In an August 14, 1980, hearing, Munro pleaded innocent to the charges.

Another accomplice lands in jail

On August 22, 1980, Gregory Matthew Miley was arrested in Houston, Texas, on two counts of murder, two counts of robbery and one count of sodomy.

He'd fled to the Lone Star State as soon as he'd learned of Bonin's arrest, and was targeted after he admitted during a recorded phone conversation with a friend that he'd participated in the rapes and murders of two of Bonin's victims.

In his confession, Miley told homicide detective David Kusher that their first victim, Charles Miranda, was a young gay teen they'd picked up in Hollywood.

Miley said Bonin raped Miranda and he tried but failed to maintain his erection, so he then held the boy down while Bonin "tied his hands, tied his feet, then tied his feet to his hands," the detective later said in court during a preliminary hearing prior to Miley's murder trial.

According to Kusher, Miley described how Bonin pulled Miranda's shirt over his head, twisting it "like a towel" before asking Miley to hold the shirt in place while he got the tire iron.

"Bonin took the iron bar, stuck it in the shirt, and began twisting it in a corkscrew-type effect until the boy was dead," Kusher testified.

They then dumped Miranda's body and drove to Huntington Beach, where they spotted James Macabe, waiting for the bus to Disneyland.

According to Miley's confession, David voluntarily got in the van and got in back with Bonin, but soon was making "crying noises" that Miley could hear from the front driver's seat.

Miley drove "a very, very long distance, and the next thing he realized was that Bonin had this young boy down and he was strangling him, again with his shirt."

"Miley admitted that he again helped hold this boy down, but there wasn't much to holding him down because he was so small, and that he helped by twisting the shirt 'around the boy's neck a little bit' until he was dead," the detective said.

Miley then told Kusher that they disposed of the body "next to a dumpster."

Fourth accomplice catches a break

Initially, police thought that 20-year-old Eric Marten Wijnaendts, who met Bonin in prison in March of 1979 and later established a sexual relationship with him, was the fourth accomplice.

Wijnaendts was believed to have helped in the murder of Harry Todd Turner – "Bonin didn't act alone in any of these murders," one of the lead prosecutors said – but he was released when police learned that it was actually their informant, William Ray Pugh, who had assisted in that murder.

"There is now insufficient evidence to believe the defendant is guilty of the crimes charged," said Sterling Norris.

They then sought to have Pugh – who had a lengthy criminal history that included arrests for burglary, robbery and assault - tried in adult court.

Bonin enters innocent plea

During a preliminary hearing on January 1, 1981, Bonin pleaded innocent to the Freeway Killer murders.

Prosecutors – including Aaron Stovitz, who was part of the team that prosecuted Charles Manson for the notorious Tate-La Bianca murders, and up until Bonin thought that those murders "would be the most horrible thing we would see" – zeroed in on the manipulation Bonin used to control his accomplices, which ultimately ensured that his victims wouldn't get away.

Stovitz called Bonin "the most arch-evil person who ever existed."

Likely very few people in the courtroom disagreed with the prosecutor, given the heinous methods of torture Bonin delighted in before killing his victims.

"We know that Bonin had his group, and that they did not act independently of him," said one official. "In the cases of Butts, Munro and Miley, all came from broken homes with no strong father identification. Bonin became the father. He gave them love."

He also helped stoke their own perverse urges, said Los Angeles prosecutor Sterling Norris, who had listened to Bonin brag to police while sharing details of their debauchery.

"He was the leader, and he chose weak people he could use," Norris said. "Bonin was the torch who lit the fire."

"He has this leadership ability to get them to follow," added Orange County Deputy District Atty. Bryan Brown, who would prosecute Bonin for his Orange County crimes. "And they do what he wants them to do."

Stovitz, whose nightmares would now include Bonin and his inescapable van of death, had some advice for the people of southern California, especially those who still believed that life in the shadow of the Hollywood sign was safe.

"Is there a lesson to be learned from this case?" asked Stovitz. "Yes. I would tell children, don't accept rides from strangers, either hitchhiking or gratuitous offers, be they from girls, boys or in between. And I would tell parents, let your sons and daughters see the pictures of these murdered children."

A remorseless killer

Bonin expressed no remorse for what he had done although he did demonstrate embarrassment and regret at being apprehended. Once confronted with the evidence, he freely confessed to police.

He also offered a confession to CBS television reporter David Lopez, in hopes of snagging a life sentence rather than the death penalty.

Still, he refused to accept responsibility for what he had done.

"It was like someone threw cold water on my face listening to a guy sitting there describing to you how he killed people and why he killed people," Lopez said. "'He was an easy target, it was a game.' I asked him what happens if you don't get caught, and he said, 'I couldn't stop. I'd still be killing. I couldn't stop killing. It got easier each time.'"

Lopez also asked Bonin why he killed so many victims, and he couldn't really say. All he said was, he "liked the sound of kids dying.'"

What he didn't like was the idea of death, even though he so nonchalantly brought it for so many of his victims.

"He said he was terrified of the death penalty," "Lopez said. "He said, 'I don't want to die.'"

Butts chooses suicide over facing the music

The testimony of Vernon Butts was one of the building blocks of the case against Bonin, but unfortunately, it would never be admitted into evidence.

By early January, Butts was dead, a towel twisted around his neck in a method of death that was eerily reminiscent of the way most of Bonin's victims died.

Police said they "were certain" Butts' death was a suicide.

"There were no other inmates in the area at that time of night. All of the inmates are on lock down, an only three people have keys to that room," said Los Angeles County Sheriff's Deputy Jerry Minnus.

Still, Butts' attorney, Joe Ingber, doubted the suicide theory, and said Butts had faced numerous threats from other inmates.

"They'd say things like, 'You don't look so tough,' or 'You like to kill young boys, but you can't stand up to a man,' or something like, 'We'll punk you pretty good.' He was afraid of those people," Ingber said, adding that Butts had spoken with his girlfriend the night before his death, and she said he didn't sound depressed.

"I think the sheriff's version is a bunch of malarkey," Ingber said. "I'm not accusing the sheriff's department of anything, but what happened doesn't make much sense."

Minnus had a different story about Butts and his supposed state of mind, however.

"He was apparently very upset about the release of the transcript from the preliminary hearing, which had been held behind closed doors last months. He seemed particularly concerned that it would shock his friends and relatives."

Butts said most of the victims were strangled with their own T-shirts, but some were attacked with a variety of butcher, buck, and steak knives and one was killed with an ice pick through his ear.

Butts was scheduled to be tried July 27 on six counts of murder.

His death erased at least some of the evidence against Bonin, said Bonin's attorney, Earl Hanson.

"Now we have an entirely new ballgame," he said. "It does remove some of the obstacles that had me very, very concerned. It doesn't hurt him as much as it would if [Butts] had testified."

Still, Aaron Stovitz said Butts' death would have no impact on their case against Bonin, set to go to trial May 4 in Los Angeles County on 14 counts of murder.

CHAPTER 6:
The trials of William Bonin

Bonin faced two trials, the first in Los Angeles County, the second in Orange County. At first the two counties battled over which would try him, until finally settling on back-to-back trials.

Two of his accomplices, Miley and Munro, had already agreed to testify against him at both.

Los Angeles trial

In Los Angeles County, he was initially charged with 14 counts of murder along with other offenses including robbery and sodomy.

Bonin was cleared of Thomas Lundgren's murder because he chose to deny it, and was not charged in the murder of Sean King because he had shown police where King's body was with the agreement that it could not be used against him in court.

Two other murder charges – those of Mark Shelton and Robert Wirostek – were dropped because he had been charged along with Vernon Butts in the deaths, and with Butts dead, his testimony was deemed inadmissible, and prosecutors felt that there was not enough evidence to convict Bonin alone.

In the end, Bonin faced 10 murder charges in Los Angeles County. His trial began on Nov. 5, 1981.

"We will prove he is the Freeway Killer, as he has bragged to a number of witnesses," said prosecutor Sterling Norris to the jury. "We will show you that he enjoyed the killings. Not only did he enjoy it, and plan to enjoy it, he had an insatiable demand – an insatiable appetite – not only for sodomy, but for killing."

The evidence was overwhelming. Not only did officials have blood, semen and hair linking Bonin to the dead boys, but also avocado-colored carpet fibers that were an exact match to the carpet on the floor of his van.

"He had an insatiable appetite for this type of killing," Norris said. "He fully enjoys the whole episode."

Too, in six of the murders, the victims had been strangled using a "windlass" method that was, Norris said, "a signature, a trademark." (Bonin's signature strangulation method involved using a tire iron to twist fabric – usually clothing belonging to the victim – tighter and tighter around his victim's neck.)

"It's a nightmare," said Barbara Beihn, the mother of Stephen Wood outside the courtroom. "I can't believe it really happened, except when I go to the cemetery I know it happened."

Miley and Munro both testified at the trial, and vividly described the details of the murders in which they had participated.

Munro spoke of buying burgers with the money they'd found in Stephen Wells' pockets.

For his part, Miley described hearing "a bunch of bones cracking" as Bonin strangled one of his victims.

And although the defense made an attempt to pin things on the late Vernon Butts, Norris handily shot down that theory.

"He was the leader, and he chose weak people he could use," said Norris. "Bonin was the torch who lit the fire."

David McVicker also testified, sharing the similarities between his brutal attack and those of Bonin's victims while revealing the depravity that Bonin exhibited each time he raped and killed.

Reporter goes against tradition

Norris had closed his case and was preparing to make his closing arguments when reporter David Lopez – who had won a court ruling that shielded him from having to testify for the prosecution - finally agreed to testify after learning that Bonin had been attacked in prison by other inmates, which delayed the rest of the trial. (It was originally reported that Bonin had been injured in a fall.)

Lopez set a precedent by doing something that had never been done before – testifying at the trial about the off-the-record confession Bonin had made to him in hopes of preventing the death penalty.

"I am not a deeply religious person," Lopez said. "But I prayed a lot."

As part of his confession, Bonin admitted to Lopez that if he were to go free, he would certainly kill again, and Lopez realized that he had to make sure the serial killer who prowled the streets for young boys ended up behind bars for life or dead.

After Bonin's trial was suspended over Bonin's broken nose and black eyes, "it made me realize that someone greater than me was trying to tell me something," Lopez said, and he chose to testify, sharing what many reporters would consider off the record conversations to which others were not to be privy.

"In some way, I'm personally ashamed of the way I behaved in this thing," Lopez said of his initial reticence to testify.

Even after facing an angry Bonin when he finally took the stand, Lopez said, "I feel good about it now."

Initially, Lopez's station held the information they had about Bonin, but when Lopez learned the suspected Freeway Killer had talked to other journalists, "I had very strong feelings I was going to be scooped on the story I was sitting on, and I knew I was sitting on perhaps the biggest story of my life. He told me he wanted to plead guilty and wanted me to go on the air with a story that he was going to plead guilty."

The station ran the story in June, and afterwards, police urged Lopez to tell them what he knew.

Lopez told the court about Bonin's account of Stephen Wells' death, which began with Bonin having sex with him on his mother's bed before dragging Wells out of the room to be killed elsewhere in the home, where Butts was waiting.

"Vern got real weird that night and stuck ice picks in his head," Lopez said Bonin had told him.

The newsman testified that Bonin described killing one youth by punching him in the throat. Other victims were strangled, killed with ice picks and sexually mutilated.

"Several officers said that I would seal the case shut, but they've been saying that since back in January," Lopez said. "I never knew I was so popular with the police. I thought it would be enough to name 21 names. But what they were asking me was to open my notebook my notebook is in my head and delve into everything he told me."

Bonin's defense attempted to discredit Lopez's testimony by suggesting he had paid $50,000 to police for information.

"Are you kidding?" Lopez asked in response.

Defending a madman

Bonin's defense attorneys called a wide range of witnesses to the stand, including his mother, who talked about the beatings Bonin suffered as a child at the hands of his father, the molestation that occurred while Bonin was in a detention home and her disappointment over her middle son being gay.

His older brother, Robert, also testified about their abusive father, the drinking that consumed both parents and the changes that came over William after his tour of duty in Vietnam.

His younger brother, Paul, talked about picking up hitchhikers with the middle Bonin brother, but asserted that they'd never injured their passengers.

Everett Fraser, Bonin's neighbor who had introduced him to his accomplices, said he had been shocked to learn that Bonin, a "respectful" friend who had been a guest in his home at least 50 times, was facing such charges.

Experts weigh in

The defense, which targeted the credibility of numerous witnesses, also offered testimony regarding the issues that might have contributed to Bonin's murder spree, including a lack of nurturing and abandonment as a child, which "led to confusion about the differences between violence and love," according to Dr. David Foster.

Because he had suffered from physical, sexual and emotional abuse – memories of which he blocked, but evidence of which was present, including scars for which Bonin had no explanation – that forced "a detachment and the use of fantasy and denial and more primitive defenses to protect himself."

Closing arguments

In closing arguments, Norris asked the jury to consider how Bonin treated his victims, "tying them like pigs and throwing them out like garbage," he said.

"These dump sites are part of Mr. Bonin's habits – to use those freeways to put a body some distance from where it was killed," he added. "These ligatures are a trademark, it's like signing Bonin on each and every one of these murders."

He also asked jurors to stand in the shoes of the victims while they considered the facts in the case.

"If just one of these victims could take the stand and tell you about the humiliation, the degradation of ending his life this way, there would be no question what the result ought to be," Norris continued. "Just as Mr. Bonin drove the van of death, picking up these young kids, I ask you, ladies and gentlemen of the jury, to drive the van of justice and tell him, 'Get in Mr. Bonin. Your days of killing are done.'"

On Jan. 5, 1982, the jury was handed the case. Members deliberated for six days before returning with convictions in 10 killings.

Bonin was found guilty in the killing of Donald Hyden, Steven Wells, Steven Wood, Charles Miranda, James Macabe, Harry Todd Turner, David Murillo, Marcus Grabs, Darin Kendrick and Ronald Gatlin.

"I think it's a very good verdict, a very just verdict that was fully earned by Mr. Bonin," said Sterling Norris. "We will ask for the death penalty."

"Even though there was not a guilty verdict on Sean, we know William Bonin killed Sean," said King's mother, Lavada Gifford. "There are 10 first-degree murder convictions, and that's a victory."

Bonin expects death penalty

After he was convicted on 10 counts of murder in Los Angeles County, Bonin said he expected a death sentence from the jury.

"I'd be stupid not to expect it," he said. "If it comes down that way it might be easier to handle."

And while he was anxious over what decision the jury might make, Bonin said he was relieved that his first trial had come to an end.

"It's finally over," he said.

Bonin's first death sentence

The jury in Bonin's Los Angeles County trial only had to take one vote before determining that the killer should die for his sadistic spree.

"Nobody likes to take another man's life," said jury foreman John Lang. "But we did what had to be done."

Prosecutor Norris was grateful for the jury's swift yet fair decision.

"The crimes were so horrible, so repeated, there was no other just verdict," he said. "After listing to this evidence, I think you reach a moral judgement."

Judge maintains death sentence

Superior Court Judge William B. Keene imposed the recommended death sentence, calling the crimes "unbelievably cruel" and the disposal of bodies a "revolting affront to human dignity."

"He had a total disregard for the sanctity of human life and the dignity of civilized society," Keene said. "Sadistic, unbelievably cruel, senseless and deliberately premediated ... guilty by any measure of possible or imaginary doubt."

Bonin cradled his chin in his hand as he listened.

"I'm happy with the sentence and I'll be happy when it's carried out," said Jim Wells, whose son, Steven, was Bonin's final victim. "That guy's a monster, totally devoid of human feeling, as could be noted that he sat there without even flinching."

Jurors as well were pleased with the judge's decision to hand down a death sentence. He had the option of handing down a sentence of life without the possibility of parole, but chose to impose the death penalty. He also ordered that if Bonin's death sentence was commuted to life, that each of the counts run consecutively, ensuring that he would spend his life behind bars.

"I was very happy because Judge Keene didn't let us down, for all we went through," said alternative juror Olivia Alarcon.

"I was very impressed with the judge and his statements," added Lang. "I think justice is continuing, and I would like to see it come to a conclusion relatively quickly."

Orange County trial

In Orange County, Bonin was charged with the murders of Dennis Frank Fox, Glenn Barker, Russell Rugh and Lawrence Sharp.

He was held in isolation while he waited to go on trial, which was much different than his circumstances in Los Angeles County.

"They have me in a room by myself, which is a bummer," Bonin wrote to psychologist Dr. Vonda Pelto from his cell in Orange County, where he awaited his second trial. "No one to talk to or play chess with. I hope my attorney is successful in getting a roommate for me. Ten months is too long to be cooped up in a medical isolation room all by myself."

Bonin's defense team attempted to get a change of venue because of the publicity surrounding the case.

The court answered the request as follows:

"Bearing in mind the criteria which the court must take into consideration in evaluating the pending motion, the court has made the following determinations. First of all, with reference to the nature and gravity of the offense, certainly the court can think of no offense or offenses which would be more grave than those which are pending in this particular case.

"Secondly, with reference to the size of the community, the evidence is clear that we have a community that is approximately two million people - consists of approximately two million people. Additionally, the voter registration is in excess of one million.

"The court ... also notes that the panels now drawn also consist of both people who have registered to vote, and, in addition thereto, we also draw from people who have obtained driver's licenses that may not be registered. Consequently, it is the court's determination from those facts that the pool which would be available is in excess of the number of people who are registered to vote.

"...Obviously this is a case that has commanded a great deal of media coverage both by television and newspaper ... [but] I don't have any evidence as to who watched what on television, what channels they watched, if in fact they do watch, what newspapers they take, if in fact they take any newspapers, and what effect, if in fact they do take newspapers, anything that they might have read has had upon them.

"In this case, the court does note that there has been a minimum amount of publicity regarding this case, at least since the imposition of the sentence in Los Angeles County.

"The court, in taking the totality of the evidence that has been presented, makes a determination at this time that there has been an inadequate showing that the defendant is likely not to receive a fair trial in Orange County.

"I think based upon the size of the community, that there is undoubtedly a large group of individuals who either have not heard about the case or if they have heard of it, heard so little that in no way is the defendant not going to be able to get a fair trial in Orange County.

"The motion for change of venue is denied."

Bonin's second trial began in March of 1983.

The trial was especially hard on Rugh's mother, Sandra Miller, who attended every day.

She had started drinking the day Orange County detectives knocked on her door to tell her that her son was dead, and had trouble stopping afterwards.

During the trial, her alcohol intake escalated, especially since her family members didn't want to talk about Rusty, and she needed desperately to remember him. So after the trial ended for the day, she would stop off at a local bar.

"I would get drunk and all I'd talk about was Rusty. It was the only time I dared to. I had so much pain," she said.

It was made worse by the empty bedroom that was Rusty's that she saw each morning after she woke up. The family had purchased a new home about a month before his murder, and he had picked out the bedroom he wanted for his own. It was a room in which he never had a chance to sleep.

"Bonin created most of our problems," said Miller. "He created a real havoc in our world."

Bonin's mom Alice Benton again testified, and said her son was nothing but kind.

"If he had a bag of candy, he gave it away," she said. (Clearly, Alice Benton had never heard the one about kids not taking candy from strangers in vans.)

Prosecutor Bryan Brown got right to the point in closing arguments.

"Bonin is a very intelligent individual who goes to great lengths to avoid leaving any evidence," said Brown. "One could truly say from the evidence found in the van it's a virtual death wagon."

"Bonin would suggest they have sex with the hitchhikers then kill them by binding them and strangling them" Brown said. "Killing to this man is less than stepping on an ant. He truly is a mass murderer."

Bonin's attorney, William Charvet, called two witnesses, one of them James Munro, who said that Bonin had contacted him through the air vents in jail, and offered him "a lot" of money to lie on the stand.

On August 26, 1983, after a six-week trial, a jury convicted Bonin on all four counts of murder.

They deliberated for two and a half hours, then determined that Bonin should die for his crimes.

Superior Court Judge Kenneth Lae upheld the death sentence.

"We're grateful," said Jerri Fox, whose son Dennis was one of Bonin's Orange County victims.

Bonin later protested what the judge said when handing down his death sentence after two days of deliberation on the part of Bonin's jury.

"He told me I was sadistic and guilty of monstrous criminal conduct," Bonin told Pelto. "I don't think he had any right to say that to me. I couldn't help myself. It's not my fault I killed those boys."

Bonin uses up all his appeals

After his trials were over and he was convicted, Bonin used every tactic available to him to appeal his death sentence.

In his appeals, he hired new lawyers who would say that trial attorney William Charvet was incompetent for failing to put more focus on Bonin's mental illness as well as the sexual abuse Bonin himself suffered as a child.

"Petitioner maintains that if Charvet had conducted a proper investigation, he would have learned that petitioner was physically abused as a child, was sexually assaulted by a number of adult males, and suffered from a bipolar mental disorder. Petitioner speculates that the presentation of this information would have humanized him in the eyes of the jury and would have made it reasonably probable that the jury would have opted for a life sentence rather than death," according to court records.

The court did not agree, and used transcripts of the trial to prove that Charvet did in fact address Bonin's childhood traumas.

"The Court finds that Charvet presented a constitutionally adequate portrayal of Bonin's childhood. During the penalty phase, Charvet presented evidence that petitioner's father had a history of abusing alcohol, gambling, and physically assaulting his wife and children. Charvet also presented evidence that petitioner was sexually molested while at a detention center when he was only ten years old. Moreover, after focusing primarily on Bonin's ability to function productively in prison, Charvet stated in his penalty phase closing argument, 'I'm not going to go into trying to blame — about the beating of the mother or losing the home — because that's not really part of it. We are talking about what happens. If Mr. Bonin lives, what happens? And why should he die?"

Bonin also said Charvet should have called more experts to testify, especially based on the determination by Dr. Jonathan Pincus, a neurologist at Georgetown University Hospital, that he suffered frontal lobe brain damage which generally causes people to be impulse driven, suggesting that Bonin couldn't control himself when he got in the van with a mission to kill.

Pincus described Bonin's excitement in the hours prior to a kill, which the serial killer viewed with the same anticipation as a child sees Christmas.

"Bonin had no insight into his reasons for doing this and he was obviously embarrassed by the details and ashamed," Pincus said. "He described feeling excited by the prospect of killing someone, of being barely able to wait for sundown so he could begin to cruise to pick up someone for this purpose and obtain some sense of release."

But he also was a bit confused by his obsessive desire to kill.

He was, Pincus said, "a fairly open, honest, reasonably intelligent person who seemed legitimately puzzled by his predilection for sexual encounters which culminated in murder."

Later, his money gone, public defenders attempted to block the execution by suggesting Vernon Butts was the mastermind, and Bonin only went along for the ride.

"They needed to have someone made the devil, and that person was Bonin," said James Ramos. "We acknowledge legal responsibility as being an accomplice, but it is our position that he did not do these murders."

For Sterling Norris, there was no question that Bonin was the devil.

"His almost universal way of killing was to put a T-shirt around their throat, use some kind of device like a jack handle to tighten it and then to squeeze," he said. "He would let them fade in and out of consciousness. These were kids. And they were not just killed, they were killed in such a gross way."

Bonin also used his knowledge of unsolved murders as a bargaining chip, but authorities weren't in the mood to play.

Still, it would take 17 years for the U.S. Supreme Court to determine that there would be no more stays, no more appeals, and during that time, Bonin played cards, wrote letters to some of his victims' family members – in one, taunting a mother by telling her he loved killing her son the most, "because he was such a screamer" – and dabbled in art, producing a book of short stories ("Doing Time: Stories from the Mind of a Death Row Prisoner") and paintings that went on display in a Seattle gallery.

"That much extra life is more than they deserve," said Bryan Brown. "We've done everything in our power to guarantee their rights. It's time to pay up."

Accomplices also pay

Bonin's primary accomplice, Vernon Butts, was dead from suicide, but his other minions – James Munro, William Pugh and Greg Miley - were facing potential sentences of life behind bars.

Munro pleads for second chance

At Munro's trial, held March 15, 1982, his attorney, James Goldstein, suggested that Munro only participated in the murder of Stephen Wells because he was afraid of William Bonin.

"I would indicate to the court that I do feel that Mr. Munro, although not being guilt free, has also been a victim of Bonin, as well as others, in Bonin's crimes. By way of emphasis, I remind the court that Mr. Munro also, at one point in time, came very close to being a victim - in the sense that he too was tied up, and that his life was almost taken by Bonin," Goldstein said. "Mr. Munro has stated this to the probation officer, and he has also maintained with some consistency, that the only reason he participated in the acts that he did was out of fear of Bonin."

The judge responded quickly and tersely.

"The court understands that, but the court finds no excuse at all for the type of conduct that this defendant has participated in. I think he should, every few seconds, say a prayer that he is not going to the gas chamber with Bonin. For what he has done - I would have no problem sending him there. So I think he is very fortunate. "

The Michigan native was sentenced on April 6, 1982, to 15 years to life for the second-degree murder of Steven Wells. He has appealed his sentence repeatedly, and is currently incarcerated at Mule Creek State Prison. Wells' parents attend his parole hearings to ensure he isn't released.

Still, he tries to plead a case for release.

"Since 1980, I have sat in prison wondering if someday I will get out, or would I spend the rest of my life in prison. I do understand, after years in prison, what I did was wrong. But do you all out there honestly say - he is guilty of murder, or was I in the wrong place at the wrong time. Yeah, I was, and I for some reason got caught up in this case. There is not a day that goes by that I don't think about what has happened, and how sorry I am for my actions. All I want is my life back."

It's a wish the families of Bonin's victims – so many of them forever unknown – likely wish every single day of their lives, but it is one that can never come true.

Munro also has written several online accounts about the events leading up to his arrest, each one a little bit different than the others, but each essentially suggesting he was a victim, even when he could have taken action to save the life of Steven Wells.

In one, written in third person, he credited himself for the ultimate arrest of William Bonin, despite the eyes police already had on the killer.

"He said that if it wasn't for Munro running away Bonin would be still on the streets killing people. When Munro got away Bonin was mad and got so mad he took his anger out on another victim, but he got caught because he tried to kill by himself. Bonin stated to reporters, 'If Munro would have stayed with me, they would have never got me,' and 'Yes, I would have killed Munro, but in my time.' Bonin was finally executed in 1996 in San Quentin, and Munro sits in prison hoping someone out in the free world will understand him and share their concern."

Miley also gets life sentence

As part of a plea deal, Miley – whose family members said was mentally disabled – was sentenced in Los Angeles County in

February of 1982 to 25 years to life for his role in the murder of Charles Miranda.

His Orange County sentence for the murder of James Macabe was the same, although it was to run concurrently with his previous sentence.

He could have received the death penalty, but he agreed to give up Bonin, resulting in the life sentence that included the possibility of parole.

He was initially up for parole after serving 16 years and eight months, but that parole date came and went.

He is currently incarcerated at the California Substance Abuse Treatment Facility and State Prison in Corcoran, where he regularly breaks prison rules.

According to officials at the facility, Miley has racked up 26 violations of prison rules, including making threats against an inmate, attempting to engage in non-consensual sodomy, refusing to attend classes, possession of unauthorized drugs, failure to comply with grooming standards and others.

Because of his inability to follow rules in the controlled environment of prison, Miley is unlikely to be paroled.

The last time Miley was up for parole, Orange County District Attorney Tony Rackauckas called him a "significant threat to public safety," which was especially apparent based on the number of violations of prison rules Miley has racked up in recent years.

Accomplice who gave up Bonin goes to trial

On May 9, 1981, William Pugh – whose story helped cement the theory that William Bonin was the Freeway Killer - pleaded innocent to charges related to the murder of Harry Todd Turner.

A year later, on May 17, 1982, Pugh was sentenced to a six-year sentence for voluntary manslaughter in the case of Harry Todd Turner.

Charges of sodomy and robbery were dropped.

He could have received a life sentence if convicted of murder, but the jury took into account his role in the capture of Bonin, which effectively ended at least one serial killer's reign of terror in California.

Jurors deliberated for five days before handing down the verdict.

Pugh would be out in less than four years since he had already served 894 days awaiting his trial.

"Bonin would still be on the streets if not for Billy," said Pugh's attorney, Edmond Barrett.

Public defender tries to get death penalty off table

As part of Bonin's appeals, public defender Monica Knox attempted to show that it was wrong to expect that the members of Bonin's Orange County jury were without prejudice in his second trial, given the publicity surrounding his first.

"The notion that a juror can say, 'Yes, I've read about the search for this guy and that he may have killed up to 44 people altogether but I can set all that aside' is unrealistic," she said, adding that the evidence compiled was "not overwhelming" against Bonin.

Her request was denied.

Do they play cards in hell?

In 1990, Vanity Fair went to San Quentin Prison, and Mark MacNamara wrote about a Death Row game of bridge, played by four inmates using homemade cards.

Bridge requires four players on two teams, and in this game were "Freeway Killer" William Bonin, "Scorecard Killer" Randy Kraft, who was convicted of killing 16 men (and was sometimes called the "Freeway Killer"), Doug Clark, one of the two-man "Sunset Strip Killers" team, convicted of killing six, and Lawrence "Pliers" Bittaker, who tortured five with pliers, he favorite method of torture.

The foursome met daily, and played for about four hours.

According to MacNamara, "They didn't much like one another, but they did like the game."

CHAPTER 7:
The execution of William Bonin

California governor Pete Wilson called Bonin "the poster boy for capital punishment."

His crimes were considered so heinous that police officers who processed Bonin's crime scenes as well as victims' families were eager for the man who dumped his victims like so much trash to draw his last breath.

They had waited almost two decades for karma to exact its revenge.

Lethal injection replaces gas chamber

In 1992, the state of California determined that the gas chamber was considered "cruel and unusual" punishment following the execution of Robert Alton Harris.

They decided then on lethal injection, and that would be how Bonin died.

It would not come as a surprise, though, if the families of his victims wished that Bonin's execution was twice as painful as Harris', described in detail by the Los Angeles Times:

"At 6:07 a.m. by the warden's watch, the pellets dropped and the colorless gas began to invade Robert Harris. He just sat there, looking forward, hangdog. The first sign of death's beginning was a twitch of his hands, as if the rising gas had stung his skin. He inhaled and exhaled, four or five times. His head snapped back. His eyes rolled into his head. After 30 seconds, his head dropped, but he strained against the straps. Then his head rose as if by convulsion, then fell forward, slowly.

"After a minute, his hands appeared relaxed. A vein that runs the length of his forehead bulged, then looked as if it would burst. His mouth was wide open. His face flushed, then turned almost purple.

"He seemed oblivious at this point, perhaps two minutes into the execution. But then, as his body seemed to have relaxed, his head rose slowly and eerily. At 6:11, there was a cough, a convulsion, a line of drool. His balding pate was visible, as was his tightly banded and short ponytail.

"By 6:14 a.m., the body no longer moved. We the living shifted from foot to foot. Light filtered in through the blinds on three windows that look out to the east. At 6:21 a.m., the three hanging lights brightened."

At 6:22 a.m., Harris was declared dead. His execution had taken 15 minutes.

Bonin's death day comes

On the day of his execution, February 22, 1996, Bonin was placed in a special holding cell on Death Row, where he was given access to his spiritual advisor, a Catholic chaplain.

One wonders if he expressed any feelings of remorse at this time, although given how he taunted the distraught parents of his victims, and claimed none of it was his fault, it's unlikely.

One of his lawyers, who continued to talk to Bonin after his dual death sentences, agreed.

"I have not detected any remorse," said former Bonin defense attorney Todd Landgren, who spoke to Bonin regularly. "It hasn't come up."

In truth, the only remorse Bonin did express was his failure to become a pro bowler, since he'd excelled at the sport as a teen.

He told a local radio station that he had "made peace" with dying, although he has no idea how he would feel when it finally came time to die, something he had feared the most after his capture.

"As far as how I'm going to feel at that very moment, I can't answer that question," he said. "I don't know. I don't think any of us would know until we're there."

He offered nothing for the families of his victims, no remorse, no apology, no hint of regret.

"I don't think anybody in a situation such as I'm in - whether guilty or innocent - no matter what they said would help in any way. I really don't," he said. "They feel my death will bring closure, but that's not the case. They're going to find out."

Last-minute fight for a stay

A little more than an hour before Bonin was set to be executed, the U.S. Supreme Court refused to hear his last-ditch plea, bringing to an end the appeals process that had lasted more than a decade.

Earlier in the day, a panel of the U.S. 9th Circuit Court of Appeals in San Francisco also rejected Bonin's request for a stay, and chose not to hear his claims.

"We've done our very best, and we think appropriately and adequately. We will not give Mr. Bonin short shrift," said Chief Justice J. Clifford Wallace.

The panel agreed unanimously that Bonin's attorneys should not have waited until the last minute to present their arguments for overturning his death sentence.

"There is no serious question of Bonin's guilt," Wallace wrote in a 19-page order, and "no fundamental miscarriage of justice" would come as a result of his execution.

The lawyers from the public defender's office claimed that Bonin's trial lawyer was incompetent, that prosecutors had withheld evidence and that witnesses had lied while judges in both trials overlooked what they saw as grave miscarriages of justice.

The panel found no evidence to back those claims, and passed the case on to the nation's High Court, which refused to hear it.

His last meal

At 6 p.m. on the day he was executed, Bonin was moved from his cell to a death watch cell, where he watched "Jeopardy" and ordered his last meal, which consisted of two large sausage and pepperoni pizzas, three pints of coffee ice cream and three six-packs of Coke. He ate alone.

According to witnesses, he appeared resigned to his fate.

"He's communicating well and seems relaxed," said San Quentin spokeswoman Joy Macfarlane.

Later, he was allowed a handful of visitors who spent his last hours with him, including one of his public defenders, James Ramos, his biographer, Alexis Skriloff, and former San Quentin guard Ben Aronoff, who hugged Bonin goodbye.

"I told Bill I loved him more than anyone I had ever loved in my life," Aronoff told the Los Angeles Times. "It was a beautiful moment."

Bonin apparently showed two sides that were a complete dichotomy. On one hand, he failed to tell the families of his victims that he regretted what he'd done, and instead almost taunted some of them with his memories of their loved ones, while on the other, he was seen as a caring, loving human being.

"He has a very basic sense of caring," said Skriloff, a Louisiana woman who is writing the book "Beyond Control," which explores Bonin's damaging childhood. "I know that's completely the opposite of what everyone sees."

According to Skriloff, those close to Bonin saw a side of him that was never portrayed by the media, never mentioned in court transcripts, not shown in the actions of one of the most prolific and sadistic serial killers in United States history.

"We saw the inner child in Bill," added Skriloff. "The child in him never got to live. He was a very caring, very giving person."

(A former neighbor, Dolly Sanders – a bartender at the neighborhood hangout the Ric Rac Pub – told the Los Angeles Times about the night Bonin sat with her in the hospital when she believed her son was going to die. "He didn't want to leave me alone," she said.)

Ramos later told reporters that Bonin stayed calm as his execution neared.

Afterwards, the three reflected on Bonin's troubled past.

"He was faced with so many significant hurdles when he was young that made it virtually impossible for him to be a successful human being," said Ramos.

The way some people saw Bonin begs the question – how can a monster who casually killed so many young men, robbing their families of a lifetime of memories, so easily wear two faces?

In his final statement, given to the warden one hour prior to his scheduled execution at midnight, Bonin again expressed no remorse for his crimes and left a note that stated: "I feel the death penalty is not an answer to the problems at hand. I feel it sends the wrong message to the people of this country. Young people act as they see other people acting instead of as people tell them to act. I would advise that when a person has a thought of doing anything serious against the law, that before they did, they should go to a quiet place and think about it seriously."

It meant nothing to the families of the boys he had killed, and did nothing to humanize William Bonin for those who did not consider him a friend.

Editorial protests empathy for Bonin

For Rob Morse of the San Francisco Chronicle, there was no excuse for William Bonin.

"Bonin was abused as a child. The abuse seems to have been bad, but not nearly as gruesome as the abuse he dealt out," Morse wrote in an editorial that went live at 4 a.m. Feb. 20, 1996.

"The world is filled with articulate people who can write and paint and were abused as children. Very few of them become serial killers. Very few become evil.

"To call Bonin's evil a 'psychiatric disorder,' as the defense has, or an 'illness,' is to slander the mentally ill. The crime rate among the diagnosed mentally ill is lower than among so-called normal people. Serial murderers like Bonin seem normal except when they're killing people.

"It's best to call it evil. It's most effectively treated by lifetime incarceration or death. An execution, whether by gas chamber or lethal injection, is a killing done in our name, and we should give it a lot more thought than eating red meat.

"Personally, I've come and gone on the issue, and I have to admit a lot of it has to do with who's up for execution. Many believe that the state has no right to take a life. This is a comfortable belief for those who don't live in Oklahoma City, don't remember Nuremberg and never had a child murdered.

"The death penalty is mainly about vengeance, or setting the soul at ease - not illegitimate motives. Relatives of victims I've talked to live in a special hell knowing loved ones are gone, while the murderers are painting pictures in prison.

"Relatives of Bonin's victims, who have been mentally tortured by his actions, are coming to San Quentin on Friday to bear witness to the death of their children's physical torturer.

"Carl Wood, the brother of victim Steven Wood, won't be coming. He committed suicide.

"That makes 15 young men who died because of William Bonin. Killing Bonin won't bring them back, and it may not ease the pain of relatives. But justice is about making hard choices.

"If Bonin's victims had lived, they'd range in age from 28 to 35. Lord knows what accomplishments he stole from them. Instead we have to read about their killer's sensitivity, his painting and his writing. The word 'rehabilitation' has been heard. Sorry, the man resigned from the human race. I don't want to pay his room and board until he goes to hell.

"It would be nice if we could shoot Bonin into space and never have to execute him. Unfortunately, we can't get off that easy."

Witnesses anticipate justice

"I just can't wait to see him take his last breath," said Sandra Miller, whose 15-year-old son, Russell Duane Rugh, was waiting at a bus stop to go to work at a fast-food restaurant when Bonin's van rambled by.

She expressed regret that Bonin's death, unlike her son's, would be painless, along with a hint of rage that Bonin's time spent in prison awaiting execution lasted longer than her son's short life.

"He actually lived longer there than my son got to live his life," she added. "Is that fair?"

Miller's son, who went by the nickname Rusty, was opposed to the death penalty, and had written a paper on the death penalty in school. The piece was among a stack of things she received from school after her son was killed.

"He believed that anybody who killed anybody ought to be helped," said Miller, who all the same wished Bonin dead for taking her son from her and upending her family.

"I think his feelings would be different if he'd known he was going to die like that," she added. "I had the perfect happy family. After this, it was like the whole world fell apart."

Another mother, Sean King's mother, Lavada Gifford, had written to Bonin for years in hopes of reading his words of remorse, but they never came. Before his execution, she wrote again to ask him if he had any last words.

To her, he did not.

Rape victim relishes his chance at retribution

"I'm looking more forward to this than anything in my life," David McVicker told the Los Angeles Times. The disc jockey from Santa Ana traveled with friends in a Winnebago travel trailer to witness the execution of the man who continues to haunt his dreams.

"Sometimes I wake myself up yelling," McVicker said. "Imagine going to sleep and getting raped 10 to 12 times a night."

It is those images, the ones that come to him when he is asleep and again at his most vulnerable, that drew him to watch Bonin's execution.

"I have to see it," he added. "It will change the mental videotape in my head. I can see him dead. I can see his body carried out. He can't rape me anymore. He's dead."

McVicker brought along a magnum of champagne and a carefully selected musical playlist, AC/DC's "Highway to Hell" and Oingo Boingo's "Dead Man's Party" among them, to mark the occasion.

"It has nothing to do with partying or getting drunk," McVicker said. "It's symbolic of our closure. It's not a ceremony, but a ritual. It signifies a new time. This is going to end it. End it. Throw me forward. I'm so ready for this. This is the beginning of my life."

Execution

At 11:01 p.m. prison guards called the telephone company to get the official time and to double-check that the phones in the death chamber were working in case the governor called with a stay of execution. The syringes and other medical supplies were already prepared and in the chamber.

With his execution scheduled for 12:01 a.m., Bonin was walked from his holding cell into the execution chamber at 11:45 p.m.

He did not struggle – according to some reports he had been given a heavy dose of Valium - and walked himself to the table where he would die, said prison spokesman Vernell Crittendon.

It would take eight minutes for technicians to find a vein for the IV, and although officials said no tranquilizers were given to Bonin, when the curtain opened at 12:09 a.m. and witnesses were allowed to see inside the execution chamber, it appeared as though Bonin was almost asleep.

"If he had any knowledge of what was about to happen, he didn't show it," wrote Mark Gribbon of Trutv.com. "With the strong dose of tranquilizer in his system, he certainly didn't care. Stoned on state-sanctioned Valium, Bonin was strapped to a hospital gurney in the refurbished California gas chamber and pumped full of three different chemicals.

"The first, sodium pentathol, a.k.a. 'truth serum,' rendered him unconscious in about a second. The next dose, pancuronium bromide, paralyzed his muscles and made it impossible for him to breathe, much like curare in a South American Indian blow-gun. The final dose – potassium chloride -- came a few seconds later and instantly stopped his heart."

By 12:13 a.m. William Bonin was dead. It took five minutes for him to die.

A reporter said his face turned purple and his chest heaved once or twice and it was over.

Bonin, number 322 – the 322nd murderer executed in the United States since 1976, the first in California to die by lethal injection - was 49 at the time of his execution. He was the first person to be executed by lethal injection in the history of California.

He had been on Death Row at San Quentin Prison for 14 years, behind bars for 17 years.

None of his family members attended the execution, and no one was on hand at San Quentin to claim Bonin's body, which was later cremated.

Not enough satisfaction

According to Los Angeles Times reporter Ken Ellingwood, many of the witnesses to Bonin's execution were disappointed that they were not allowed to see the entirety of his death.

"The scene was so sterile it was hard to remember a man was meeting his death," wrote Ellingwood afterwards. "Behind a white curtain in the converted gas chamber, William G. Bonin lay face-up, strapped to a table, his arms implanted with the tubes that would carry the poison to his veins. The 50 witnesses who took their places around the windowed enclosure did not see Bonin's final walk. They did not see the expression on his face as he entered, or the prison technicians who struggled several minutes to find a usable vein.

"When prison guards pulled open the curtain, Bonin, in fresh denim clothes and gray socks, blinked at the ceiling, his belly rising and falling as the trickle began. His mustachioed face betrayed nothing. If he was making a sound, none escaped the sea-green steel bubble. After about 50 seconds, Bonin's chest heaved twice, quick as hiccups, and he puffed hard, exhaling his final breath. A minute later, his skin was blue."

"I'm not sure what we witnessed," said Sam Stanton from the Sacramento Bee.

And San Francisco Chronicle reporter Kevin Fagan described the event as "less involving than watching a vet put down a dog."

In response, the California Department of Corrections said that they weren't hiding the execution process from the public, but instead were protecting those who led the killer into the chamber.

What people wanted, of course, was the fear – no, the sheer terror – that Bonin's victims suffered, and that "eye for an eye" was not what they got.

"I think it was really a humane execution," said Bernie Esposito, a detective who was part of the task force that finally nabbed Bonin in June of 1980.

Still, family members of victims had expected more than watching Bonin's peaceful trip into that good night.

"I feel like, man, they still cheated us. We didn't get to see him even get strapped down. I didn't get eye-to-eye contact. I didn't get to see him walk in," Miller said. "We didn't get anything out of it, other than his death."

Victims' families change face of execution

According to Annulla Linders, a University of Cincinnati associate professor of sociology, allowing the families of victims to observe executions has made people see executions in a different light.

"I argue that the opening up of the witness box to the murder victim's family has turned the execution into a somewhat different kind of event than it was – it has come to re-personalize executions and re-infuse them with interestedness and passion," she said at the 2014 American Sociological Association's annual meeting. "No longer is it enough that the death is swift and the arrangements are efficient, the execution must now also satisfy the psychological demands of long-suffering relatives and other intimates of murder victims."

Capital punishment is now thought of more as a way to exact retribution on behalf of victims and their families, she said, rather than as a deterrent to crime.

"The family members of murder victims are in the witness box to view and judge something other than the execution of the law," she said. "They are there as survivors, not so much to observe the execution – there are official witnesses to do that – as to bear witness to the pain and suffering experienced by murder victims and those they leave behind."

The aftermath

While Bonin waited for his date with death, he kept himself busy, at one point divulging some details of his crimes to Vonda Pelto in hand-written letters to the psychologist.

His words revealed the depth of his depravity, and likely made Pelto breathe a sigh of relief when Bonin was officially dead.

"At one time the guy asked, 'Why are you doing this?' I have no answer. Just before he went unconscious, I let up and asked him, 'Do you want to know why you have to die?' He said yes, and I said, 'Your folks paid us to find you and kill you.' Then I pressed down on him again and he was finally dead.

"I took the rope off of him and took the ice pick and stuck it up both nostrils and into his ear. This was to make sure he was dead. We then drove out to the freeway ... and finally found a place and dumped him, fully clothed, down into an irrigation ditch. Then we got back onto I-5 and drove back to Los Angeles."

An error in judgement

In 2004, Munro was back in the news when he attempted to pin the 1979 murder of 13-year-old James Trotter on Bonin during the pretrial hearing for convicted child molester James Lee Crummel, who was charged with the crime after telling authorities he'd found bones while hiking in Cleveland National Forest. Munro later recanted his testimony.

Initially, in an interview taped at the prison where he was housed, Munro said he would "remember it the rest of my life," and told officials that Bonin had described Trotter as "the easiest one he killed."

In court, however, Munro said it was "a lie. It was payback to Bonin for ruining my life ... for the hatred I have for that man. I didn't realize how much trouble I'd get in by saying that."

Munro later said he learned details of Trotter's murder in a 1996 news story that ran after Trotter's bones were identified, and decided then that if he was ever asked about Trotter's case, he would say that Bonin was the assailant.

Give me death

Munro also captured attention by writing to then-California Governor George Deukmejian, asking to be executed on his birthday.

"I came into this world on June 17, I might as well leave it that date," Munro told the Los Angeles Times.

The first time, the governor's office wrote back, pointing out the futility of such a request.

He wrote again. This time, Governor Pete Wilson did not respond.

"I feel for the Wellses, I really do," Munro said of the parents that attend every one of his parole hearings to prevent him from being released from prison. "I wish I could tell them face to face how sorry I am for what happened to their son. That's why I want to be executed, to show them I'm willing to give up my life to make all this easier on them."

In truth, he wants to make it easier on himself.

"I would rather die than to serve more time for a crime I didn't commit," Munro said.

Planning a second killing spree?

Munro comes up for parole from time to time, but it is unlikely that he will ever be released.

There's Steven Wells' parents, for one thing. Then there's Munro himself, who hasn't gotten any smarter during his time behind bars.

According to Vonda Pelto, Munro is getting reckless, and has said in interviews with her that he wants to kill again, "to finish Bonin's work."

Pelto has been around enough prisoners to know whether or not she should take his words seriously, and despite Munro's previous attention-grabbing acts behind bars, this time she was concerned.

"I think he's a real threat," she said. "He really wants to do this so he'll be in the newspapers. I asked him: 'What are you going to do when you get out?' And he said: 'I'm going to continue Bonin's work.' In other words, continue killing. And that's when I asked: 'Well, do you have anybody in particular?' And he says he has a list. And that's when he said David McVicker was high on the list."

She immediately alerted McVicker – the rape victim whose tip helped police zero in on Bonin (although an offered reward was withheld from him) - and he made plans to attend a 2014 parole hearing for Munro, who serves as a vivid reminder of a nightmare he just can't seem to shake.

"I'm a victim. I shouldn't have to be doing this," McVicker said. "But it's not over until these guys are gone. I've kind of taken it on myself to make sure that justice is served and they all stay in jail ... just not on the streets to go and do it again."

When Pelto learned during that telephone call with Munro that there might be someone on the outside working with Munro and Miley – he told her that this person had already purchased a van similar to Bonin's and was ready to start a new spree as soon as the two were out of prison – she reported him to the California Department of Corrections and Rehabilitation, too.

Investigators found that on the outside, an accomplice had established a fake Facebook account that was being used to harass the families of Bonin's victims in an attempt to prevent them from testifying at the parole hearings for Munro and Miley.

They also made close contact with McVicker.

"He's threatened to kill me," McVicker said of Munro. "I've had three phone calls that I know of coming out of prison in the past week, that he was threatening to have me killed by tomorrow. The thing that's really scary about that is they actually went to my house."

In attempting to track the owner of the account, investigators focused on William Harder, a self-proclaimed serial killer junkie who operates a website selling murder memorabilia and had spoken with both Munro and Miley several times.

No criminal charges were ultimately filed against Harder, but police also never determined who was behind the intimidation, or whether or not that person had a van.

The information, however, led them to reject Munro's bid for parole in 2014 after a four-hour hearing. That means he won't be eligible for parole again until 2029.

McVicker told the Orange County Register he was "very, very happy."

CHAPTER 8:
Bonin's terror lives on

For the families of the victims of William Bonin and his accomplices, Bonin's execution did little to erase the trauma of losing their sons or brothers.

Those families now realize to what extent evil lives in the world, and they are reluctant to venture into its territory.

"Now I stay home all the time," said the mother of one of Bonin's victims. "I'm paranoid, I don't go out after dusk. The only thing that gets me out of bed is my hobbies, like crochet and painting. People say time makes things easier. Well, I'm still waiting. I wish I could be happy. I just can't find my way out of this maze."

Secrets went to the grave

The mother of one victim who disappeared during Bonin's reign of terror and whose bones were found near Ortega Highway pled for Bonin's execution to be stayed just one more day so he could be asked about her son, but the governor of California couldn't be reached.

"He was out of town. We tried up until two or three minutes before the execution," said Barbara Brogli, who lost her 14-year-old son and felt certain that Bonin was responsible. "I would like to know, definitely. It would be a complete closure. If he did do it, the man's been punished and he'll be dealt with at a higher level. For quite a while, I've been really praying to find out, to know whether he's dead or alive, and I've been praying for strength to get through it. I really believe my prayer was answered and God will take care of the rest."

DA searches for DNA to complete Bonin's sordid portfolio

Carol Burke of the Los Angeles County district attorney's office is fairly certain that William Bonin is responsible for more murders than the 14 he was convicted of – or the 21 to which he had confessed.

She's hoping to get the DNA to prove it.

Burke heads a project called Dead Man Talking which uses DNA evidence to link cold cases with known felons, even those who are no longer living.

"There is a lot of value to it, even though we can't prosecute the offenders because they are dead," Burke told the Daily Beast. "Families can at least have some closure. They finally know what happened to their loved ones."

Amazingly, Bonin's DNA is not part of California's databank, and no swabs were taken before he was executed and cremated, his ashes then tossed into the Pacific Ocean.

"He's my number one target," Burke said. "He was a really bad guy. He was so prolific."

Tracking down DNA will be difficult, because his court files and trial evidence have been destroyed, and none of the police departments involved in tracking Bonin took or saved blood, semen or saliva samples.

But Burke is not giving up.

"Bonin is the most notorious and the one who most likely left unsolved murders in his wake," Burke says. "It sure would be great to get his sample so we could solve some of the unsolveds out there."

Mother reaps financial bounty during Bonin incarceration

Several weeks after Bonin's death, California officials learned that Bonin's mother, Alice Benton, had used her son's Social Security payments – issued for a mental disability – to pay $75,000 on the mortgage of her Downey home. Those payments should have ceased in 1982 when he went to prison, but a glitch kept them coming.

It wasn't until a funeral director alerted the Social Security Administration that Bonin was dead that the agency realized its mistake.

The family agreed to pay back the $75,000.

The other Freeway Killers

The first serial killer to carry the nickname the Freeway Killer, Patrick Kearney, turned himself in to Riverside, California, police on July 1, 1977.

He had been on the run for two months after evidence linked him to the murder of 17-year-old John LaMay.

Kearney confessed to killing 28 boys and young men, dismembering most of them and discarding the remains in trash bags. (Because of this particular M.O., he was also known as the Trash Bag Murderer.)

Three years after the arrest of William Bonin, Long Beach, California, police arrested 38-year-old Randy Steven Kraft, who was linked to murders dating back to 1972.

His method of disposal was similar to Bonin's – he tossed them out like so much trash on the side of the road – but Kraft drugged many of his victims, and his methods of torture included burning the young men he captured with the cigarette lighter in his car.

The three Freeway Killers - Bonin, Kraft and Kearney – may be linked to as many as 131 victims.

A movie merges truth, fiction

In February of 2010, "Freeway Killer," a film directly based upon the murders committed by Bonin and his accomplices, was released by Image Entertainment, creators of the movie "Dahmer." Scott Anthony Leet starred as William Bonin, while Dusty Sorg played Vernon Butts.

Leet, a method actor, spent months researching the character and his back story – especially so the ongoing childhood abuse that led to his murder spree – and gained 35 pounds and dyed his hair black to play the role. When he walked on set, he was totally immersed in his Bonin character – and totally frightening, allowing him to revel in putting his co-stars and others on the set completely on edge.

He talked about his experience with the hosts of "Without Your Head" Horror Radio.

"The thing that was outstanding about William Bonin, the first thing you notice, was what a hair trigger temper he had," Leet said. "It was an interesting character to play because of that hair trigger factor." "At the drop of a hat, this guy had no conscience. Rape and murder for William Bonin was a total addiction."

Leet was also interested in how easily Bonin was able to appear normal during the times when the desire to rape and kill wasn't consuming his thoughts.

"He fit into society better than most serial killers. He was like a regular guy," Leet said.

Still, playing the role of someone so inherently evil was exhausting, despite the relatively short five-week shoot.

"Honestly, it does take a toll," Leet said. "Playing William was extremely difficult. It was bloody and brutal, to relive what this guy did. He's heinous. Once you're in that character and playing it, to a certain degree it's spiritually debilitating. It was a difficult shoot, to say the least."

Leet wished that the directors had left some of the meat of the story intact, such as the molestation as a child that eventually influenced Bonin's sexuality.

"They cut a lot of his backstory out of the movie, and that really disturbed me," Leet said. "William was a hell of a character, and I think that backstory he had, going through that life, made him who he was. I will definitely carry it with me for the rest of my life," he said.

The movie is available on DVD and Netflix.

Conclusion

While hitchhiking has slowed considerably, the highways and byways that crisscross the United States are still peppered with people looking for a new life or their next adventure.

But there are still a lot of William Bonin's out there, abused as children and ready to take it out on the next person to get inside his or her car.

I'd take Aaron Stovitz' words to heart, and find another way to reach your destination.

A Note From The Author

Hello, this is Jack Rosewood. Thank you for reading William Bonin: The True Story of The Freeway Killer. I hope you enjoyed the read of this chilling story. If you did, I'd appreciate if you would take a few moments to post a review on Amazon.

Thanks again for reading this book, make sure to follow me on Facebook too see all my new releases and deals!

Best Regards
Jack Rosewood

Printed in Great Britain
by Amazon